DIFFICULT PEOPLE MADE EAS

Nancy Slessenger
Vine House essential © 2003

Difficult People Made Easy
Copyright © by Nancy Slessenger 2003

Published by Vine House essential Ltd

ISBN 1-904611-03-6

Author: Nancy Slessenger
Editor: Jo Parfitt
Project director: Charlie Hall

Designed and produced by Hullabaloo Visual Communications Limited

Dedication

For Jane and Hugh, thanks for suggesting the idea in the first place.

About Nancy Slessenger

Nancy Slessenger is Managing Director of Vine House – a consultancy which focuses on helping organisations find practical solutions to complex people problems. Nancy is the author of many publications including "Brain Magic" which she co-authored with Andy Gilbert. As a conference speaker Nancy enjoys helping delegates find out what goes on inside their heads. As a facilitator and development specialist Nancy uses the latest brain and learning research to help individuals, teams and organisations to increase their communication skills, effectiveness and performance.

www.vinehouse.co.uk is a natural extension of this passion – to provide a place for people to learn and further their personal and business development.

How to use this book

If you are interested in difficult people

I have done my best to give plenty of examples of each type of difficult person. This will help you to identify the types of people you are dealing with and makes the book easier to understand. Once you have read about the six types of people I cover here, you may want to test yourself by doing the quiz at the end of the book.

If you have an immediate problem

In this case you need to do your best to identify the kind of person you think you are dealing with. Then you can skip straight to the summary of that chapter and check the list of behaviours to look out for. If they fit, go on to read the corresponding chapter as well as the tips on what to do and what not to do.

If you are keen to learn

If you do not have a specific need, but want to learn more about dealing with difficult people, then jump ahead to the quiz at the back of this book. There is at least one question for each chapter. Have a quick look at the questions before reading through the book, keeping the questions in mind. Do your best to find the answers while you are reading.

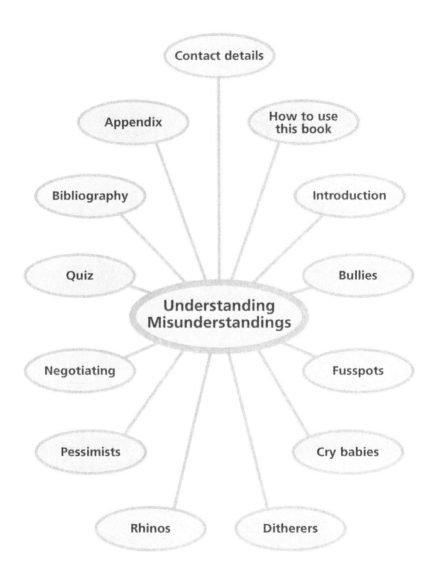

Contents

Introduction

Many years ago I went to America to take a one-week training course. The course was excellent. However, after two days surrounded by people I hardly knew, who were hugging me as if they had known me for years, being an English person I needed some quiet time on my own. My hotel fee included three meals a day, but in spite of the extra outlay, I decided that the only way to get some peace without forfeiting any of the training was to pay for breakfast somewhere else. Somewhere quiet. I wandered down to the harbour and found a small breakfast bistro.

The bistro served people who were going out to fish for the day.

The building had been constructed like a huge glass triangular prism. Through the large clear glass windows I saw a dark and almost empty interior. There were functional tables seating six and a row of stools along the bar area.

The menu looked good. There was a large selection including various options that meant nothing to me. There was something called Granola which I have since learned is a kind of muesli. There were pancakes with syrup and bacon, which sounded tasty, and there were also 'breakfast burritos'. I had never come across anything like that, but made a mental note of them and promised myself I'd try them the next day if they looked good.

I walked in and took my place at one of the stools by the bar. The only other customer sat at a table on the other side of the restaurant. I was sure sitting so far away from him would be a signal that I wanted to remain undisturbed. The very helpful waitress took my order and brought me a fresh orange juice, in a glass the same size as my medium saucepan. It was delicious.

When I say 'fresh' I mean it was squeezed directly from a large number of oranges. This was quite unusual in England at the time. It was the best orange juice I had ever tasted.

At last I had some peace and time to reflect and catch up on the latest copy of New Scientist. I had barely glanced at the editorial when I sensed another customer entering the establishment. I was not concerned; after all, there were ten empty tables and probably fifteen empty stools. There was plenty of room for another person to eat without disturbing me.

The new customer came and sat on the stool immediately to my left. I couldn't believe it. I carried on reading. He turned to me and, in a voice that would easily have carried to the customer on the other side of the restaurant, happily announced: 'Hi, I recognise you. You're on the Brain-Based Learning course, aren't you? You're Nancy. Pleased to meet you, I'm Raleigh.'

I was mortified. How could this person dare to interrupt my little haven? 'Have you ordered yet?' he continued. 'You must try the breakfast burritos – they're fantastic.' And he smiled a huge, friendly smile, to reveal glistening white teeth.

I confessed that I had ordered and was looking forward to the pancakes and bacon.

'They're good, sure enough, but the burritos are better,' he told me in cheerful loud tones.

Seeing that my quiet hour had been ruined I decided to join in the conversation Raleigh was so determined to have. Believe it or not, this turned out to be one of the most fortunate meetings of my life. Raleigh became a dear friend and introduced me to many other wonderful people. Even now, many years later, he and his friend, Lew, still send me information about research and conferences I should be attending. Ironically, these conferences have helped me immeasurably in my work with difficult people. How could I have classified Raleigh as a difficult person in those first few minutes? Because that's exactly what I did.

The key is lack of understanding. Raleigh is a naturally friendly person who behaves in a very American way. I doubt if I even register on his scale of friendliness. I misinterpreted his friendliness as brash rudeness (I have revised my opinion since!). He was also right about the burritos.

In dealing with difficult people, I have noticed that many of the problems arise out of someone misinterpreting someone else's actions or behaviour. Usually, when people are able to understand others more effectively, the situation changes. The reason it changes is because our behaviour towards the other person changes – and that, in turn, changes his or her behaviour.

Let me tell you another story. Near the start of my career, I was running a department for a manufacturing company, located on a different site from the rest of the organisation. We weren't far from the main building, but we might as well have been in another country from the number of visits we received.

Then, one day, we had the worst kind of visitor. The Safety Officer, known as Old Jim. He must have been in his late fifties and was also exceedingly grumpy. He was well known for his constant complaints about things that weren't really problems at all. We production managers thought he made people's lives very difficult. Old Jim never seemed to have a kind word for anyone.

I spotted his crumpled figure doddering round the corner at once. I knew he hadn't seen me, and seriously considered hiding behind some racks. Then I decided that would be just too childish and thought I should try something else. In a split second, and for no particular reason, I decided to imagine he was someone I really liked. I picked an old school friend I hadn't seen for years but who would be very pleased to see.

I rushed up to Old Jim with a big smile on my face.

'Jim, how kind of you to come and see us,' I trilled. Grabbing his elbow I steered him towards my desk. 'You will stay for a coffee, won't you?'

Old Jim opened his mouth to protest.

'Please,' I pleaded, to the astonished looks of my team. I moved my battered chair over and sat him in it (we didn't have much furniture).

Before he could say a word I carried on.

'You take black without sugar, don't you?' I rushed off to the machine and bought two coffees and hurried back to Old Jim.

I found a broken chair behind a bench and carried it over to my desk. 'We don't have many visitors,' I explained apologetically. 'In fact, you are the first to come for ages, probably this year.'

Old Jim had still not uttered a word.

'It's so good of you to think of us. Now, what can I do for you?' I said, my smile now permanently painted on my face.

He was so stunned at this approach that he just sat on the chair opening and closing his mouth like a goldfish. His false teeth wobbled slightly in a rather unattractive way.

I seized the initiative again. 'Now you're here, you will come and say hello to everyone, won't you? They'd be so disappointed if you went off without talking to them,' I insisted.

I dragged him up and wheeled him round the department. My team was amazed and clearly thought I had lost my marbles. However, as old Jim walked around, he showed genuine interest in what they were doing and people seemed pleased to talk with him.

I finally let him go – but only after he had promised to come to see us again in a few weeks' time.

So the visit was a success. In fact it was much more of a success than I realised. Old Jim did me several favours over the years. He never once complained about anything I did again and supported me in many other ways too. He was in control of one or two useful resources and I always got more than my fair share of them. Several of my colleagues asked me what I had done to deserve such perks.

That episode made me realise that we are ourselves responsible for creating many of the problems we have with other people. We have much more control than we think. We just need to know how to use it.

For years I have found the area of difficult people fascinating. I have worked with many clients, some of whom I have helped to deal with a difficult person; others have been the so-called difficult person. Sometimes I have worked with an entire team of people.

Over the years I have discovered that virtually all these difficult people are doing the best they can under the circumstances. In all this time I have only met one person who quite deliberately made life unpleasant for others. The rest did it without any effort on their part at all.

In general, people have no idea how much their behaviour upsets others or causes difficulties. How many times have you discovered that something you said was taken the wrong way or caused offence that you did not intend?

In working in this field I have done my best to find ways for people to work together more easily and happily. I haven't always succeeded, but have always learned something from each encounter.

This book is to help you to deal with the kinds of people you find difficult in a way that will make your life easier.

It is divided into chapters, each dealing with a specific kind of difficult behaviour. Over the years I have encountered many similar situations, so whilst all the examples I use are real in some way, they are often compiled from three or four similar situations. I have changed the names, contexts and sometimes the sex of the participants. But each example, although not an accurate description of one specific incident from start to finish, is itself based on real people and problems.

As time has gone on, and I have attended more conferences and training courses, I have discovered and developed more efficient ways to resolve these problems. I will continue to do so and have my friends Lew and Raleigh to thank for that.

Each chapter concludes with a summary of behaviours for you to look out for, and suggests your best course of action. I also include a little on the theory behind each behaviour. Use these summaries to help you understand the misunderstandings you encounter in your personal and professional lives.

And next time you are faced with a close encounter that you don't quite understand, remember that sometimes people who seem to be difficult turn out to be your most valuable friends and supporters.

Nancy Slessenger
www.vinehouse.co.uk
October 2003

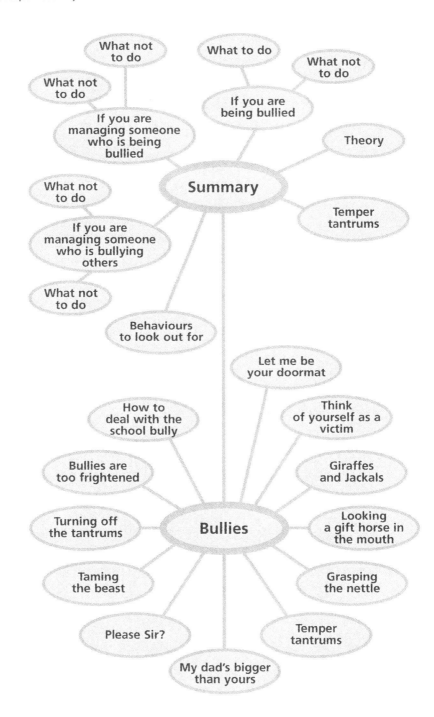

CHAPTER ONE

Bullies

Understanding bullying people

I was asked to see Miranda, a woman who was clearly very stressed. We had arranged to meet in a small, plain office at 10am. The day was grey and dull as I waited for her to arrive. Miranda was ten minutes late and came into the room looking pale and drawn. She was in her fifties, a small mousy woman with grey hair and gold-rimmed glasses. Her skirt was grey and she wore a pale blouse with a cardigan in another light colour. She looked like the drab woman in that advertisement, the one who had been using the wrong washing-powder and all the colour had been washed out of her clothes.

I introduced myself. After asking if she wanted a coffee, I asked Miranda to talk about what had been happening. She started to cry convulsively. She gulped as tears streamed down her grey cheeks. I got her to move around, which seemed to help a bit, and tried again to ask what had been happening – with the same result.

As Miranda spoke, I could hardly understand a word she said. I managed to discover that she used to do quite a bit of singing, so I got her to remember what she knew about breathing. Then I led her through some exercises and she started to calm down a little. I tried again to find out what the problem was – with exactly the same result. She sobbed convulsively. This went on for nearly an hour. This was the worst case I had ever seen. Usually I am able to help a person to relax and begin talking about the problem within five or ten minutes at the most. Not this time.

After an hour and lots of breathing exercises, Miranda was finally able to gulp out the story of her manager, John, whom she said was bullying her terribly. She described how he didn't trust her, was constantly looking over her shoulder and shouting at her. She started to cry again. We took a break and talked about the music she used to sing.

She told me how John did not care at all about her needs. He made her work through breaks and he made her work many extra hours. He criticised her in front of others, calling her stupid and careless. She found this particularly hard to take because she cared deeply about the work that she did.

Miranda said John was rude, he never asked people to do things, he just told them. He never checked whether it was convenient for them or not. He changed the rota without consulting people and, in her view, deliberately put people on shifts that were difficult for them.

She was in such a bad state that all I was able to do during this first session was to teach her a strategy parrot-fashion. I told her that, for her next encounter with John, she must go to him rather than wait for him to come to her.

Let me be your doormat

Here's a bit of background. When you feel someone is bullying you, you tend to avoid him or her. This is only natural. Often though, this means they will end up coming to you, especially if they have to as part of their work. The problem with letting the other person come to you is that he inevitably arrives at the worst moment, when you are least prepared. Also, because of previous encounters, you spend most of your time worrying about when this person is going to 'attack' you. This puts you at a huge disadvantage. When you go to him instead, prepared and ready, the interaction can be a great deal easier.

I gave Miranda the words to use:

'John, here is the report you asked for. Please let me have any changes you need by Friday and I will have them completed by Wednesday afternoon.'

We practised the interaction many times until she could say it clearly and firmly with a smile and at least *look* confident, even if she did not feel it. I could not begin to imagine how difficult this would be for her.

And off she went to put what she had learned into practice that very afternoon. We agreed to meet again a week later. As I walked through the rain back to my car, I couldn't help worrying how she would cope.

All week I wondered how Miranda had got on. I was hoping she had managed to complete the phrases in a clear strong voice. Or at the very least, say them out loud.

The following Wednesday Miranda met me in the same room. She was a different woman. Her face had colour in it and her clothes looked brighter.

'I did what you said and John was totally different. He just said: "Yes, OK",' she told me.

Not only that, but John had returned the report to her as agreed and there had been very few corrections needing to be made. Miranda had completed them early.

'I can't believe it,' she kept repeating. 'All the time it was me!'

Miranda was quite stunned by this revelation. Reflecting on the dramatic change in John's behaviour, Miranda had worked out that if she could change his behaviour so substantially by changing her own, then she must have been having a negative impact on him in the first place and therefore had to be responsible for having been bullied.

Naturally it was very upsetting for her to think that for the past ten years she had been the cause of her own suffering.

For many people, perhaps not you, this is a very controversial idea. I've got into trouble before for putting it this way. But the evidence I have seen leads me to the conclusion that, in many cases, a person's behaviour leads him to be *bullied*. If you think back to your school days, I bet you knew who was going to be bullied before it happened. You could often tell by the way a person walked that he was more likely to be a victim of bullying than other children. Now that's not to say that the bully has no responsibility. Of course, no one should treat others in this way. But it becomes a great deal easier for someone to bully others when people behave like victims.

Think of yourself as a victim

Over the years I have noticed that there are sets of beliefs and behaviours that can (but don't always) lead to a bullying situation.

Do you catch yourself thinking: 'I'm only... ' As in 'I'm only a typist', 'I'm only a mother' and so on?

Seeing yourself as something insignificant while others hold lots of power is another sign.

Worse still, do you ever catch yourself believing that others are responsible for your situation – that is, blaming others for the way you feel? Watch out for phrases such as 'You *make* me feel...', 'He *made* me feel angry/unhappy', 'I feel *squashed*' and so on. These are signs that you may not be taking responsibility for your own situation.

Abdicating responsibility and blaming others can mean that you then start assuming that there is nothing you can do about a situation. In my view, there is always something you can do. Even if we look at research on illness we find that people who believe they can play a part in their own recovery get better more quickly than those who don't (or indeed, get better compared to those who never recover).

Giraffes and jackals

Many years ago I was fortunate enough to see Marshall Rosenberg speaking at a conference. He has done a great deal of work in this field of bullying. He talks about Jackal Language (this is the language of blaming others, or violence) and Giraffe Language (this is about speaking with heart). He picks Giraffes because they are known to have very large hearts.

I immediately bought his book, *Nonviolent Communication*. In it, he lists the feelings that tell us when our needs are being met: feelings such as happiness, delight and gratitude. He then outlines feelings that tell us when our needs are not being met: feelings such as sadness, edginess or hostility, for example. Then there is a third category, and it's a real surprise. This category is reserved for a set of feelings that he says are not feelings at all; they are ways of blaming others for the way we feel. These are words like *bullied, neglected, patronised, misunderstood, let down, disappointed, betrayed* and so on.

This whole concept was a revelation to me and gave me a new way of understanding how people thought about themselves and others. The impact on a person's behaviour is resounding. When you encounter someone who is not taking responsibility, the first thing you have to do is to find a way for him or her to start doing that.

It seems that, until a person does take responsibility, he won't take action to resolve the situation. Why should he? It's so much easier to sit back and blame someone else. One of the words I have learned to become particularly sensitive to is should. For example: *He should not treat me like this. Or: He should give me some respect.*

Marshall Rosenberg suggests re-phrasing using the structure:

'When you shouted and said my report was rubbish I felt angry because you did not seem to have any idea what the report was about or how much effort I had put into it.'

Instead, many people use something along the lines of:

'You are bullying me. You shouldn't do that.'

Or:

'He squashed me when he said...'

The first phrase takes responsibility for the situation. The other two are ways of blaming others.

Another big problem that impacted on Miranda and John was detail-orientation. There is nothing wrong with being able to handle detail. Our bookkeeper was hired because she is particularly good at this (and because I'm not!). It means she does a great job at noticing my mistakes – so she's never short of work. The key is that you need to have the flexibility to be able to see the big picture too. It's when you can't see the big picture that the problems start.

In the next chapter about detail-orientated people, or Fuss Pots, I ask you to imagine looking at the world through a long cardboard tube, like the inside of a toilet roll, but longer. I ask you to think about how difficult it would be to navigate using just this device. Another difficulty caused by this view of the world is that any problem you encounter fills your whole mind. So all you are aware of is the problem.

The problem tends to get blown up out of all proportion. Worse still, you can't see any solutions. There is much more about this in the chapter on detail-orientated people. For now, just imagine what it was like for Miranda. She had made what for her was a huge step. I was very pleased (and relieved). By chance, and totally unrelated to all this, she had been headhunted for another job. It was a more senior position than her current one, and better paid too. At the same time her company was closing the department where she currently worked. They were offering positions in other departments but alternatively, a very generous voluntary redundancy package.

Looking a gift horse in the mouth

Miranda had not even considered taking the redundancy package. I asked her why she just didn't take the money and run. It seemed like a gift to me. Her response was startling.

'Because he would have won,' she said. Miranda was so consumed by this conflict that she could not recognise a golden opportunity when she was handed it on a silver platter. Her face was twisted and her eyes were hard and small. 'He's not going to beat me.'

'Do you want to be happy?' I asked her.

There was a pause. A strange look overtook her features. I waited. She took a deep breath. It was as though this thought had never occurred to her. She had spent so long in the deep, black pit of despair that she couldn't easily think about being happy.

'Yes,' she replied eventually, looking confused.

'Well, why not call these people?' I suggested.

'What would I do at the interview when they asked about John?' she asked.

'How would they know?' I continued.

Again a very long pause.

When a person is living in a very detailed, small world, he or she does not tend to be able to see things from other people's perspectives. In fact, I don't think they are even aware that other people may *have* a perspective.

There is more on this in the next chapter.

Eventually she conceded that a future employer was not likely to know about John and so would be very unlikely to ask.

Miranda was living her life by avoiding what she was frightened of, rather than striving for what she desired. It's a very stressful and sad way to live.

We had two more sessions, Miranda and I. During each one I worked with her on how to be interviewed and how to relax. We spent time focusing on what she wanted out of her life. She had spent so long focusing on what she *didn't* want that it took quite some time for her to do this.

And then, a few weeks later, she called me to say she had been offered the job and was taking it. A few months later I received a card from her to say she was very happy in her new job and how she wished she had done this ten years ago. I was delighted.

What was less impressive was the response of her company to the situation. I had been called in by the HR department to work with Miranda. All sessions that I conduct with any client are completely confidential as far as the content is concerned. I will sometimes explain the techniques I have passed on to someone, but never the content. In this case I was very concerned about the behaviour of the manager. Of course, I had only heard one side of the story, but I felt that some investigation at least was required.

In cases of bullying, the 'victim' is often very reluctant to take any action for fear of reprisals. However, I knew the HR manager well and decided to have a word with her. I said I had been working with Miranda and that I was concerned about the behaviour of her manager, John, from what I had heard. As it turned out, the HR manager was more than aware of the problem. She had counselled against recruiting John in the first place.

Unfortunately John's manager did not want to take any action. This is quite a common problem and usually stems from the fact that people just don't know how to deal with it so they do nothing. Often, even the manager is frightened of the bully. This leads to the problem being perpetuated and to others being bullied. The costs can be extreme.

Grasping the nettle

But that wasn't the end of the story in this case. By a strange chance, I met Miranda's ex-manager, John, when I was running a workshop on coaching. As I looked down the delegate list, his name leapt out at me. Naturally I was intrigued.

Even before people had introduced themselves, I had guessed which one was him. John was a rather short man and slightly overweight. His hair was thinning and lay plastered back flat on his head, held there by some kind of cream (either that or it was very greasy). His clothes were greasy-looking too and his complexion was white and taut. He looked tightly wrapped, like a grubby parcel.

From the expression on his face, he was not enjoying himself. His face whispered it, and his body shouted it. His fists were clenched like conkers and his shoulders were tense and unyielding. Small patches of red peppered his bleak forehead. He looked like a man who had been born wearing the ill-fitting glasses he constantly fiddled with.

I put him in with a group of managers I knew quite well for the role-plays and kept a close eye on that group. His behaviour was extraordinarily aggressive. He seemed unable to see anyone else's point of view and kept shouting at his colleagues. He seemed to be constantly on the point of eruption.

The other managers in his group had a lot of trouble getting him to carry out the exercise effectively. I went over to help them. John was telling the rest of the group about a 'stupid woman' who had worked for him. This woman was slap-dash in her approach and careless in her work. She never did what she was told to do and was lazy, he told his astonished colleagues. I knew he was talking about Miranda.

'How do you know?' I asked him.

'Her work was rubbish,' he said, stating his opinion as though it was a fact.

'In what way was it rubbish?' I asked.

'She never did what you told her to do. She was always going home early instead of finishing her work. She was just bone-idle.'

'Did you try to find out what the problem was?' I asked.

I asked one of the other members of the group to play the woman we agreed to call Jane.

'Let's imagine you have a report you need her to write,' I proposed. 'Show us how you would ask her.'

'Write this report and don't make any mistakes,' he barked. The others were aghast. I asked them for comments.

'That seemed rather aggressive,' one of them remarked. John looked surprised. He clearly did not understand.

'Have you tried asking instead of telling?' I enquired.

'What do you mean?' he almost shouted at me.

I asked Richard, another manager in the group, to show us how he would handle the situation.

'Jane, I have a report that needs writing by Friday on the XYZ project. Would you have time to do it by then?' said Richard.

John looked confused. He really couldn't see why he should ask rather than tell.

'How can I run a department if I have to keep kow-towing to my employees?' he asked. He was completely unaware of the needs of his employees and saw asking as a sign of weakness.

I tried several approaches to help him that morning; nothing made much impact. He really needed some individual help.

At one point, he criticised me behind my back in a rather unpleasant way to Elaine, one of the others in the group. I knew her well and had worked with her before. Over coffee, Elaine told me what had happened and asked me how she should respond when she next encountered John. I thanked her and said I'd deal with it myself.

I approached him over lunch. Predictably he was sitting on his own, as none of the others wanted to sit with him.

'John, I understand you are unhappy with the way I am running the course,' I said in a clear, measured tone.

He looked at me, alarmed. 'No, no, it's fine.' There was a note of fear in his voice.

'John, I have just spoken with Elaine and she told me that you had voiced your concerns to her. She told me so I could do something about it.'

'Oh, I didn't mean you. That's not what I meant at all.' He back-pedalled furiously.

'John, please tell me what you would like me to do differently and I'll see what can be done,' I said.

We eventually sorted the problem out without any nastiness or bullying. He had not understood one of the key points and also found the whole concept of coaching very hard to understand. He couldn't see why you didn't just tell people to do things. Most of all, although he didn't admit it, I think he was frightened of looking stupid in front of colleagues. Discussing this was very difficult for John. He seemed terrified.

I couldn't help thinking how dreadful life must have been for Miranda, all that time she had been working for John.

In most cases like this, if you confront the bully he will back down completely. The trouble is that most of us don't confront the bullies in these situations, so it never occurs to them that there is a problem with the way they are behaving.

It is very important to deal with this kind of behaviour as soon as possible – the longer you leave it the worse it is for all concerned. And it's important it is dealt with correctly, not in a way that blames them or threatens them.

Most so-called *bullies* are people who are frightened and have poor communication skills. They are people who don't know how to get others to listen to them without behaving aggressively. They need some help. Unfortunately, most people don't know how to help them either, or how to respond to their behaviour, and all too often it goes untreated.

Temper tantrums

Another client, Geoff, phoned me in desperation one day after a meeting some of his colleagues had been through with his client, a man called Andreas. They were working on a long and complex project. In order to keep to the agreed schedule they depended to a great extent on information coming from the client at specified times. As often happens, this information had been delayed. There is a procedure for this kind of situation. You re-draft the contract, talk to their contracts department about it and the outcome is usually fine. This time it was different.

They had worked with the contracts department and understood from the contracts people that all their suggestions were acceptable. They then had a meeting with the project manager, Andreas. The project manager told them the delays were unacceptable, tore up the new contract and threw it in the bin without even looking at it. He shouted and raged at them and Geoff's colleagues left without agreement.

Geoff called me as soon as he heard. He was concerned about the contract and wanted to know what he should do. I asked him to describe Andreas's behaviour and what Geoff's colleagues had done. They had been so surprised that they had not really done anything apart from leave with their tails between their legs.

Geoff wondered if he should attend the next meeting himself. Now, Geoff has three children. I asked him how he thought the client's behaviour compared with his children's behaviour. I heard him laugh.

'It's just like Lucy,' he said.

He went on to tell me about an incident just that week when his four-year-old daughter had been in a supermarket with his wife. Lucy had wanted a chocolate bar. His wife had told Lucy that she could not have a chocolate bar. Much to his wife's embarrassment, Lucy had then thrown a tantrum in the middle of the supermarket. I asked Geoff whether his wife had given in. He told me that she had not. They had a very clear policy on tantrums and bad behaviour in their family.

I asked Geoff how they intended to follow the situation up with Lucy. He said that his wife had already spoken to her about having chocolate in future. She must ask for it nicely, saying 'please', and if she wasn't allowed to have one at that particular time then that had to be an end to the matter.

'So how do you think you should treat Andreas?' I asked.

'Can I really treat him like Lucy?' he asked.

'If you want to make any progress, that is exactly what you need to do,' I replied.

The question here is: *What is the message that you're giving someone when you allow him to get his own way through bullying?* The message Andreas gets is that bullying is allowed. So he will carry on doing it.

With bullying, you need to draw some clear boundaries and then stick to them. You also need to meet the needs of the bully. Very often these needs are just to know that someone has listened to him. In the fascinating article 'Negotiating without a net – a conversation with the NYPD's Dominick J. Misino', which appeared in *The Harvard Business Review*, Misino describes his strategy when dealing with hostage-takers. It seems that hostage-takers have very much the same need that our project manager had here: to be listened to.

We can use exactly the same strategy as Misino uses. You need to listen to what the bully says and summarise it using his language and intonation. Never say you understand exactly how he feels or what it must be like for him. That can be extremely insulting: I doubt if any of us really knows how anyone else feels. Using someone else's language and summarising what they've said back to them is a clear message that you have listened. When you are dealing with someone who really needs to be listened to, you have met his needs simply by listening. You don't even have to agree with what he has said.

Geoff wondered if he should go to the meeting himself or whether he should send his managers. And now we come to another interesting perspective on bullying behaviour.

My dad's bigger than yours

Bullies tend be very hierarchical in their view of the world. People who are more senior are given more respect. Sometimes this behaviour can seem almost pitiful. You may wonder why this is. Let's think about how we develop our negotiation skills.

When we are very young, during our first few years, we don't have many linguistic skills. So if we want something we have to point at it and hope someone else will give it to us, or we have to grab it for ourselves. This is bullying behaviour. It is the first negotiation skill that we learn. When we are very young, it is entirely appropriate to use this behaviour.

Most people then develop their skills further. They move on to bartering. If you have children you may have noticed the phrase *'it's not fair'* comes in around the age of five. Other favourites include *'she's got two so I should have two'* and *'he can stay up till eight, why can't I?'* These are examples of bartering behaviour.

As we grow further, we learn more advanced negotiation strategies – or most of us do. Often, people who rely on bullying behaviour have failed to learn other ways of getting what they want or of meeting their needs. It's like having a very old radio without an effective aerial. When you can't get a good reception for the station you want, you just turn up the volume. It works, but not very well. What you really need to do is get yourself a more modern piece of equipment.

The problem when dealing with someone who is still using bullying behaviour well into his adult years, is that your eyes tell you that you are dealing with a grown-up person. Your ears, however, are telling you that you are dealing with a five-year-old. This is quite a confusing message for your brain because those are two conflicting signals. Your brain goes with the signal from your eyes so you keep using strategies that work well with grown-up people, but are incomprehensible to five-year-olds.

When you are only five years old, everyone who is bigger than you has more power than you. Believing that *bigger = more powerful* is very sensible, and it's backed up by lots of evidence. As you get older (and taller) this becomes less and less true. Most people change their beliefs accordingly. But not everyone. Like Andreas.

I suggested to Geoff that he should go with his colleagues to the next meeting with the project manager because he was more senior than they were and this would give them an advantage. The strategy would still work if he didn't go but this was a very important contract and he wanted to use every tool available to him.

I told Geoff to listen carefully to what Andreas said and wait till he had finished. Then Geoff should summarise it back to him using Andreas's own words, and wait for a response. Once Andreas had agreed that Geoff had correctly summarised what he had just said, Geoff could carry on.

The next step was to explain, calmly and clearly, exactly what he could and could not do, when he could do it by, and how much it would cost. I warned Geoff to expect another tantrum from Andreas at this point. Geoff was not to worry at that stage; he was just to repeat the process until it worked.

Later that week Geoff called to tell me about the meeting. He told me it had gone exactly as I'd predicted. The project manager, Andreas, had ranted and raved; Geoff had summarised and explained what he could do; Andreas had ranted and raved a second time. Geoff had summarised again and then told Andreas exactly what he could and could not do, giving budgets and timescales.

'Is that your final offer?' Andreas asked meekly after the second time.

'Yes,' said Geoff.

'Oh, OK then,' replied Andreas.

Geoff told me later that his colleagues had been both amazed and impressed.

This is very similar to the response from many bullies in other comparable situations.

In one of my first jobs as a consultant, I worked as an associate for a large consultancy – XYZ Consultants Ltd. I was working on a project run by Francis, one of the directors. Francis behaved very much in this fashion. One day Francis managed to upset a client so badly that she could no longer work with XYZ Ltd. The client asked if I could run the project for her instead of using the consultancy. Francis agreed to this and gave her my direct number. He also agreed with me that I could have access to the material that he had been planning to use with this client – for a fee.

I felt this was a fair arrangement given that the consultancy had designed the material in the first place. We agreed I would pay a certain amount each time I used that material. I then had to negotiate a new fee for the project with the client. This particular client was a very honest and straightforward woman. Within five minutes we had discovered that Francis had given us conflicting information. He had told the client that I had completely free access to the material. This meant that the client was expecting a rather lower fee then I was able to offer her.

After many previous examples of Francis's difficult behaviour, I had finally had enough and decided to challenge him. I called him from my hotel.

'Francis, you and I agreed that I would pay you a fee each time I used your material,' I said.

There was a murmur on the other end of the line, which I took to mean 'Yes'.

'I have just been speaking with the client and it turns out that she is under the impression that you have given me completely free access to the material.'

'Oh,' he stammered. There were some mumblings at the other end of the line.

I told him this behaviour was completely unacceptable and that, given that he had told the client I had free access to the material, I would not be paying any fee.

'Oh, OK then,' he said.

Surprised at his sudden capitulation, I almost forgot to say I would confirm our conversation in writing. It was only after this event, when I recounted it to one or two of my colleagues, that I discovered this behaviour was common for Francis. I also discovered that hardly anyone had ever pulled him up on it.

That's really the problem: the way the rest of us deal with these situations often encourages the behaviour that we don't want, rather than reduces it. The difficult person gets the message that it's perfectly all right to behave in that way, and no one tells him how he needs to behave.

The interesting thing here is that when you challenge this behaviour it almost always crumbles to ashes. I worked for many years with a small software company. I got on well with Jason, the MD of the company, but I was aware that some people found his behaviour rather difficult.

This was underlined for me when I was asked to run a course for some of the directors and Jason decided to come along too. I saw a couple of the others and they told me they really didn't want the course to go ahead if Jason was going to be there. When I asked them why, it turned out that they were all quite frightened of him. They were convinced that he would monopolise the workshop and ruin the experience for everyone. They also felt they would not be able to relax at all during the day.

I persuaded them to work with me on the course and told them just to follow my lead. Once everyone was there that morning, I told them I was just going to explain the ground rules. I explained that I was in charge for the day, and that people were only to speak when I made it clear that it was their turn. If anyone hogged the floor (apart from me) I would turn to them and say: *'Shut up'* and they must comply. I looked round the room and asked for agreement. I received eager nods from the other directors and managers and a shrug with a smile from the MD, Jason.

We had been going for about ten minutes when Jason started on his hobbyhorse, lecturing everyone. I turned in his direction and said 'Jason, shut up.' He looked startled and slightly embarrassed but stopped talking immediately.

His colleagues looked amazed, but relieved. I only had to remind him once more during the whole day. For the rest of the day his behaviour was exemplary. But that's not the really interesting part. The most interesting thing about the day was that at the end he came up to me, very enthusiastically, and thanked me for an excellent course, shaking my hand vigorously.

'I have always heard your courses were good, but now I know why – excellent course!' he said and disappeared off into his office.

The strange thing about people who use bullying behaviour is that they have respect for people who control them effectively. It's not even that difficult, you just need to know what to do – and do it.

Please Sir?

The most startling experience I ever had concerning someone with this behaviour was at a school. One of the department heads, Charles, had a reputation for being utterly terrifying. I understood, from speaking to the head, that all the pupils and most of the staff were afraid of him. I had only had a few dealings with him, and he'd seemed perfectly OK to me.

I was running a workshop about assertive behaviour and various communication issues for the department heads. At one point I asked Charles a question. He went berserk. He shot out of his seat, his face ablaze, and started shouting and swearing at the top of his voice. It was quite an experience. I confess I was quite startled, but at least I now understood what the others had been talking about.

Before I could respond, one of the other department heads, a small shrew of a woman called Sue, leant quietly forward.

'Charles, I thought today we had come such a long way as a team. When you answered Nancy's question like that, I realised we hadn't,' Sue said in her tiny, quiet voice.

Charles's response was staggering. He stood completely still, frozen, and stared at her open-mouthed. Every person in that room was holding their breath. The silence seemed almost solid and then he spoke.

'Thank you,' he said. 'I have always known I did this, but I never knew when. Now I do.' Charles was completely overcome with emotion. The other department heads were speechless.

I had always heard that people behaving like this don't know they're doing it, but I'd never really believed it till that moment. Let's look at why.

When you get angry your attention is focused in a very specific way. Daniel Siegel, author of *The Developing Mind*, tells us that emotions regulate the flow of information and energy. The emotion of anger ensures that hardly any information comes in, at that moment, and that information flows mainly out – usually in the direction of the person on whom the heat of our anger is focused. This means that we do not get any signals telling us how angry we are, unless we are very aware of our own emotions (quite rare in these situations). It also means that we have no idea how our behaviour is affecting anyone else.

At some time, you have probably told someone she was shouting and had the response: 'Shouting, what you mean shouting? I'm not shouting!' Believe it when I say that they *really* don't know they are doing it.

The reason Sue's comment worked so effectively was that her colleague, Charles, had no idea how he was behaving. He was quite shocked when he found out. The key is for the person to receive some feedback in a form that gets through to him. Then he needs a mechanism for dealing with the situation. He needs to learn a different way of negotiating. Most people can learn this.

The woman who cut Charles down to size so expertly was the head of the special needs department. Sue had a great deal of experience with children with poorly developed negotiation skills. She was well able to deal with children who bullied others. Sue simply used the same technique on her colleague and saw the same success.

There are two objectives when we are dealing with this kind of behaviour. The first is to handle the situation immediately; the second is to help the bully develop his skills so that, over time, it becomes less of a problem. In this case, by responding more effectively to the behaviour when you encounter it, you not only achieve your first objective, but you help to achieve the second objective and do everyone else a favour too.

In my work with many of these people, I have consistently found that they are completely unaware of how upsetting their behaviour is for others. Some are astonished when they realise how bad it is, others feel dreadful about it. Most of them are capable of learning different ways to behave, if only someone will help them.

Taming the beast

I spent some time coaching a very senior woman, Isabella, in a large corporation. She had recently been promoted and wanted to improve her management skills. A few years earlier, I had designed and run a series of courses for some of her teams. As part of that process, I had interviewed the people in the teams to discover their needs. At the top of the list was how to deal with Isabella.

Isabella was Italian and had a hot fiery temper. She had lived in the UK for many years, since she was about fifteen. She was small and wiry with a mass of dark hair, which always seemed to be moving. Her nose was long and thin and her dark eyes seemed to be waiting, ready to pounce like a cat watching an injured bird. She had a reputation for being unpredictable and that made people jumpy in her presence.

Her clothes were always smart and elegant, though I imagine she would still have looked good, dressed in an old sack. We had met a few years before when she'd asked me to design a course for her department. After her promotion she contacted me again and asked for some help.

'I need to improve my management skills,' she told me in a very straightforward manner. 'What should I do?' Isabella was rather more direct than most of my clients tend to be.

We discussed what she wanted to achieve with the department and where she saw the greatest challenges. She wanted to encourage them and was vaguely aware that some of them found her hard to talk to. I decided to follow her lead and take the direct approach.

'Some of them find your behaviour terrifying,' I said.

'No, I can't believe that,' she smiled and laughed.

'Do you remember the meeting when Deborah presented her new plan?' I asked.

'Oh, yes, but that wasn't so bad.' She pulled a face. 'Was it?'

'Yes, it was,' I said.

Isabella had told Deborah that her plan was a complete waste of time and that she should be ashamed of herself. She had asked Deborah questions about minute bits of detail, and when Deborah didn't know the answers, she had told her that she should be more prepared in future before presenting to the team. I asked her how she thought her remarks had come across to the team.

'Well, I had to put up with that when I was in her position,' Isabella retorted in her defence.

'How did you feel at the time?' I asked.

After a long pause, Isabella looked down, and in a quiet voice said: 'I hated it.'

'And how did it help you?' I continued.

'It made me what I am today. I wouldn't be in this job now if I hadn't had to fight for it,' she replied almost fiercely.

'So just because you suffered, you think everyone else should,' I summarised.

Finally she agreed that it probably wasn't necessary. 'But how else can they learn?' she asked.

'It depends what you want them to learn. Do you want them to learn to be defensive and frightened, or to think creatively and discuss things openly?' I asked.

As the session continued, we worked on other ways of dealing with presentations like the one I had described. These included asking Deborah for more information about her original research and finding out about her perspective, rather than Isabella giving her opinion straight away as though it were a fact.

She agreed that shouting insults at her team members during large meetings was counter-productive.

'But what can I do when I get really frustrated with them?' she pleaded. Isabella seemed to be softening at last.

'Take a deep breath, smile, and ask for more information till you understand how they have reached the conclusion they are presenting,' I said.

I explained that one of the key signals to look out for is when you think that you are right and the other person is wrong. As soon as you hear yourself think that, it's a warning sign that your thinking is beginning to narrow. You need to take action as soon as possible. Now you need to ask questions until you understand the other person's point of view. The measure for this is that what they have done should, bearing in mind their level of skill experience and their background, seem reasonable to you. Until it does, keep asking. To illustrate what I meant I described a situation of my own that I had completely misjudged:

When I first worked as a production manager, I had a woman working for me whom I considered lazy. Sally seemed to me to be sly and feckless, always doing as little as possible to get by. She was thin and weak-looking with big black circles under her eyes. But when it came to overtime, she was always at the front of the queue and asked me for more and more. I thought her whole attitude was appalling.

Why should I pay her to work overtime when she didn't put in any effort during normal hours? Unfortunately, because we were desperate for the work, I often asked her to do the overtime (paid at one and a half times the normal rate) against my better judgement. I was seriously thinking of giving Sally a warning for poor performance.

Then one of the other women took me to one side.

'Do you know about Sally's husband?' Freda asked me.

'No.' I said. I had no idea what she was talking about.

Freda went on to tell me how Sally had been forced to marry by her parents. Her husband was a violent man who beat her regularly. She lived with her parents-in-law and had to get up at 4am every morning to cook for them and clean the whole house. When she got home in the evening she had to do more cleaning, the washing (without an automatic washing machine!) and cook all the food. Then she had all the washing up from the meal. She rarely got to bed before midnight.

If she didn't get overtime her husband would beat her because he was losing money. She was never allowed to take time off if she was ill, because we only paid a person three quarters of their normal wage when they were off sick. In fact she was very ill. She had cancer and was supposed to have an operation to have the cancer removed. But her husband had thrown away the letters telling her of her appointment so that he didn't lose money while she was in hospital and off work.

I was mortified. I saw her behaviour in a whole new light. Sally was not lazy, she was exhausted. I knew I could never have coped with that situation.

Sometimes, once you have run out of questions, you will find that they were right all along, in which case you have saved yourself the embarrassment of looking stupid. At other times, you will spot some information that is not available to them, just as Freda did with me. When this happens, ask them if they are aware of it or if they have taken it into account. In my case, Freda had no need even to ask. I was shocked by Sally's situation and that I had never even considered that there might be some reason other than laziness for her behaviour.

Freda behaved gracefully in this situation and I was grateful. I have tried to follow her example ever since. Never behave as though you have caught the person out. It's very childish.

Over the months, Isabella put this into action. The first few times she found it difficult to curb her natural instincts – but, after a few tries, she started reporting that she was getting some excellent results. She was managing to get agreement with people on issues and she didn't have to repeat the same debate several times. Gradually it became easier.

Isabella is not an exception. She was capable of learning some new ways of dealing with people, and she was capable of understanding others. She had allowed herself to get carried away in the heat of the moment. Now that she has started to use more effective ways of dealing with these situations, she has become more productive. So has her team. She is surprised at how useful this skill is, when dealing with other senior managers in the company. Her new skills have led to her becoming involved in more of the strategy decisions.

Turning off the tantrums

What bullies need to learn is how to negotiate effectively. Here are the steps for a person who has only bullied (instead of negotiating effectively) up until now.

1 **Identify the bully's feelings accurately.** Help him to understand what he may be feeling. Sometimes you will need to give him a list of emotions to choose from. You will find a full list at the back of this book in the Appendix.

2 **Work out the message behind the feeling the bully is experiencing.** This is the unmet need I talked about earlier. Most of us could do better on this front. At this stage you need to help the person work out the need behind the want:

   I feel angry because I want to beat up Simon.

   The *need* behind this could be anything. You must find out the facts and what the need is behind the want, for example, here are some options:

   a) Simon has not completed a piece of work on time – the need may be to get the work completed.

   b) Simon has produced poor quality work – the need is probably for the work to be completed at the appropriate level of quality or to satisfy the customer in some way.

   c) Simon has not spoken to me for three weeks – the need might be attention.

3 Identify an action you can take right now that can help to meet the bully's need. Make sure that you are tackling the *need*, not the *want*.

Helping a person who has bullied others to use this process can significantly reduce the number of temper tantrums in the workplace (and improve the lives of colleagues too). After a while, people will get the hang of using these methods and be able to use them on their own.

This is very close to the Collaborative Problem-Solving (CPS) approach, recommended by Ross W Greene PhD for dealing with what he calls *Explosive Children*. I think it's worth remembering that, if an *Explosive Child* does not learn how to deal with these situations, he or she will end up as an *Explosive Adult*.

The method outlined above is also the beginning of learning how to negotiate – because first of all you need to learn how to negotiate with yourself. The next step is to find out what the needs of other involved parties may be, as well as your own. Once you all start working together on meeting everyone's needs, you are negotiating.

Bullies are frightened too

One of the strange things about bullies is that they are frightened and fearful themselves. When you feel like this, an olive branch can look like a big stick. I was once involved in a negotiation with a colleague. We spent ages preparing for it and I went through with her what would be the best language to use.

The woman we were negotiating with was every inch a bully. Serena, my colleague, was technically very skilled but had no experience of dealing with people like Janice.

Janice was tall and aggressive-looking. She had a severe haircut and a fierce temper. I explained to Serena that she must not do anything that could be seen to be even the least bit threatening. This included using the word *why*.

You may wonder how *why* could be threatening. Remember, you are dealing with someone who is behaving like a young child. When you were young, I expect you can remember your mother, father or other responsible adult asking you: *'Why haven't you done your homework yet?'* *'Why do you always have to leave your dirty clothes all over the kitchen floor?'* and *'Why can't you ever help with the washing up?'*

Were they requesting information? No. You were already guilty as charged. So, if you ask someone behaving like a young child a question like that, they will interpret it as an attack.

Unfortunately that's what Serena did.

'Why do you want this extension on the time scales?' Serena asked.

The whole negotiation had been going very well until that point. Janice exploded like a nuclear weapon. It took another half an hour before we could get any sense out of her at all.

Just in case you are wondering what Serena should have asked to get that information, here's the question re-phrased:

'What are your reasons for asking for an extension on the time scales?'

Phrased this way the question assumes that Janice does have reasons, and so is much less likely to provoke an aggressive or defensive response.

How to deal with the school bully

I went to a big, mixed comprehensive school. We had our share of bullies. They didn't usually bother me, but one day, as I made my way to a lesson, one of the most feared bullies, we'll call him Gobber, was sitting on the wall by the path with his gang.

'Oi, tennis racquet,' he shouted. I knew he was talking to me, my surname, Slessenger, is close to Slazenger, the well-known sports equipment manufacturer.

I chose to ignore the comment.

'Oi, tennis racquet,' he bellowed, and it was obvious he meant me so I had to respond.

'Sorry,' I said. 'What do you mean?' in the most innocent tone imaginable.

'Well, your name,' he said, a little confused. 'It sounds like the tennis racquet people.'

'Oh yes, I see what you mean!' I said doing my best to show genuine surprise and admiration for someone who had made such a difficult connection.

His gang were starting to snigger behind their hands.

'It does sound rather like that, you're right,' I continued. 'Thank you. It would be great to be one of them, wouldn't it?' I pointed out. 'I'd be rich. I wouldn't have to come here any more.'

'No, I s'pose not,' Gobber replied with genuine interest, and smiled. The rest of his gang were laughing openly by now.

'See you then.' I smiled and walked calmly to my lesson. He never bothered me again. In fact he used to say hello in quite a friendly manner after that.

Do you have one of those surnames? It's useful to have a response to this kind of teasing worked out ready. And if you have children, make sure they are prepared to respond effectively in a way that will de-fuse the situation. Practise it with them so that, the very first time it happens, the problem is solved. Above all, do your best to ensure that they walk and move in a confident manner and know how to make conversation with different kinds of people.

Summary

Behaviours to look out for

A strong focus on their own needs
These people do not focus on the needs of others. When they act they do not think about the cost to others. Usually they are completely unaware of it.

Negative assumptions about others
These people often refer to others in derogative terms, which assume incompetence or deliberate belligerence.

Telling others what to do
In many situations they will jump to conclusions without gathering facts and tell others what to do, rather than ask.

Exerting control over others against their will
Phrases like 'you must' and 'I will not tolerate' are common.

Blaming others for problems and events
This person does not tend to take responsibility for his or her own actions.

Opinions are given as facts
Statements like 'This is useless' and 'This is rubbish' are used instead of analysis of the situation and facts.

Personal insults are delivered in front of others
They use phrases like: 'You are an idiot,' or 'You are stupid.'

The victim tends to think there is nothing they can do
This is probably the most serious problem of all. They speak in terms of what the person does to them.

If you are managing someone who is bullying others

What to do
- **Gather the facts from the person who feels bullied** and others who have witnessed incidents. Identify what has happened on particular occasions. Make notes.

- **Also identify whether the bully is able to behave reasonably.** Has he or she acted like this in the past? Has he ever made requests in a reasonable way, taking others' needs and views into account?

- **Listen to the bully.** Ask him or her about specific incidents. Find out what his/her perception is. Do your best just to listen and ask questions without being judgemental. Often these people feel that no one listens to them. Summarise what the bully has said to show you have listened.

- **Ask him how he thinks his behaviour is perceived by others.** You will probably discover he has no idea how offensive it is. He probably will not even realise he is doing it.

- **Ask him what it is he needs to achieve.** Help him to identify the real need, rather than the 'want'.

  Not: *'I want him to do the report on time the way I say it should be done.'*

  Instead: *'I need the report to be done by Friday in the same format as the previous ones.'*

- **Ask him how else he could deal with the situation.** If you know he has behaved acceptably in other situations, you know he is capable of it.

- **If there is no evidence** of the bully making reasonable requests in the past, it is quite likely he will have no idea how to behave differently. You will have to give him a way of doing it. For example, let's imagine Fred is bullying Jemima.

  You would say to Fred:

  'Fred, when you need to ask Jemima to do something for you, here is how I want you to say it:

  "Jemima, the PVR report needs to be ready for Friday morning. Could you do it for me please? Thank you."'

  Then check that Fred has understood by getting him to ask you to do something using the structure you have suggested to him.

- **Make it very clear that the previous behaviour is not acceptable.** Explain what will happen if there are further examples of this behaviour.

- **Help the bully to feel safe.** People bullying others often feel threatened and frightened. Tell the person that you are there to help him and ask what support you can give.

What not to do

- **Ignore it.** Don't imagine bullying will just go away or get better on its own. It won't. It will get worse and will also cost you in the long run.

- **Allow your own behaviour to be lowered to the same level.** Make sure you retain the use of your cognitive abilities. Once you start to get cross with this person, your reasoning skills are drastically reduced. You need to help him to see other people's perspectives, so set the example yourself. Once you start forcing him, or making him do anything, you are using bullying behaviour yourself.

If you are managing someone who is being bullied

What to do

- **She needs to stand up to the bully.** This is usually easier to do if she approaches the bully rather than waiting for the bully to do the approaching. She needs to make clear requests and statements. Often standing up in the presence of the person doing the bullying (rather than sitting down) can make a big difference.

- **Make it clear to the person experiencing the bullying that you are supporting her** and that you have spoken with the person doing the bullying and told him that the behaviour is unacceptable. Explain to her how you expect the bully to behave in future, and that you will be checking up on progress. Make a date to do this.

- **Help the person to use the strategies below.** All the actions listed below will help. If she needs more help, or some professional advice, get it to her as soon as you can.

What not to do

- **Ignore it and hope it will go away.** I make no apologies for wording this very strongly. Being bullied can make someone's life a misery. It is vital that you help her in some way. Once you know what to do, these situations can be resolved. By not helping, you are actively contributing to the suffering of this person and must bear the responsibility for that.

- **Allow others to think this behaviour is acceptable.** By not tackling it, or not taking it seriously, you are condoning this behaviour. That is completely unacceptable.

If you are being bullied

What to do

- **Remember you are dealing with a two-year-old child.** I know this sounds ridiculous, but as soon as you realise that's the behaviour, the easier it is to deal with.

- **Get the bully's attention.** To do this, you need to use his name. Remember, his attention is much more likely to be focused on himself than on you. Bullies tend to be self-centred.

- **Repeat back his requests, using his own words.** This will let the bully know you have listened and will encourage him to change his emotions.

- **Find out what he really needs to achieve.** The bully will usually have just jumped to one solution, often an ineffective one, to get what he believes he needs. This is a want, not a need.

- **Carefully ask questions about the needs and situation.** The questions need to be showing interest, and not be an interrogation. Use what, where, when, who and how questions.

- **Ask questions to expand his understanding.** A bully focuses mainly on his own needs and on himself. This leads to many misunderstandings. To help him see others' points of view, ask him questions. (Telling a bully rarely helps, as they often don't listen.) Here are some examples:

  'What do you know about what I was doing yesterday?'
  'What do you think we need to achieve?'

- **Ask him questions about the consequences of his actions.** Use these to help him think into the future. For example:

  'What happened last time we did this?'
  'Do you think that will happen again?'
  'How much will this cost?'

- **Never use why** questions because these could be interpreted as a threats or attacks.

- **Listen carefully to his answers** and summarise them. Use his own language and intonation. Often he won't really know what he needs and you will have to help him work it out.

- **Help the bully to feel safe.** Most bullies feel threatened and frightened. A basic need is to feel safe. It's much easier to behave in an adult way if you feel safe.

- **Ignore any personal insults.** Focus on what needs to be achieved.

- **Have you been doing something he or she could perceive as a threat?** We often do this without meaning to. When you are in a position of authority it is easy to behave in a way that may come across as aggressive. This can be seen as threatening by some. Ask a trusted observer to give you some feedback.

- **Be clear about what is acceptable and what is not.** A bully needs to know what the rules are. He will keep pushing until he does know. You have to enforce the rules. When you say no, you must mean it.

- **Think about your own behaviour** if you are working with someone who uses bullying behaviour towards you.

Make sure that for your next meeting with the person:

a. The time and date are at your convenience
b. You are prepared
c. You remain standing (to give you more authority)
d. You ask the questions, such as *'When do you need this report?'*
e. You do not use the word *'Why'* (this can be interpreted as a threat)
f. You breathe deeply and regularly (this helps you to keep calm)

What not to do

- **Behave like a victim.** If you start thinking you are a victim, you will soon end up as one.

- **Blame the bully.** This means you are not taking responsibility for yourself and your actions. Once you stop taking responsibility you have lost control. Keep control of yourself.

- **Think 'I'm only...'** This devalues you and your abilities. By doing this you help the bully.

- **Get angry with yourself.** By doing this you are treating yourself as badly as the bully is. Treat yourself with care and love. Always. Be understanding and focus on improvements. Forget about any mistakes you have made.

Theory

Adults often don't realise they are playing the victim or bullying. When you were at school, you probably knew which children in your class were going to be bullied before it happened. That's because certain behaviours, such as looking sorry for yourself, whining, adopting a very submissive posture and constantly being frightened of everyone, encourage bullying – as does taking yourself too seriously. Other behaviours, such as standing up straight and standing up to bullies, discourage it.

Most children have learned more effective ways of negotiating than bullying, by the time they are five or six. A few do not, and carry on using bullying behaviour into adult life. They need to learn more adult behaviours.

When we deal with bullying behaviour, we are dealing with a five-year-old's behaviour coming from a grown-up. This is confusing. As a result we tend to treat people as if they are grown up. This does not work. We need to treat them as we would a five-year-old. We need to make them aware of their behaviour and of its effects. Then we need to help them find more effective ways of behaving.

Temper tantrums

Behaviours to look out for

A person starts shouting or losing their temper
This often happens in an unpredictable way, although they may also be entirely predictable.

Bullies rarely know they have lost their temper
They may not know they were shouting.

The bully does not realise the effect it has on others
Other people may think he is doing it on purpose. This is hardly ever the case.

What to do
- **Wait till he has finished** what he needed to say. Then summarise it, using his own language and intonation (so make it sound urgent if he did).

- **Ask him:** *'What would you like me to do about it?'* (Don't worry – it will not be as bad as you think – often he won't be able to answer.)

- **Tell him** what you can and can't do, and by when.

- **If he starts ranting again**, simply repeat the process. It will stop after two or three rounds.

What not to do
- **Interrupt while he is ranting.** There is no point. Just sit quietly and note what he says. Keep calm.

- **Give in easily.** Doing this will encourage him to do it again. And again.

Theory

We all have a tolerance level for a range of emotional responses. Once we leave our window of tolerance, we lose control of our behaviour. This is because we lose access to parts of our cerebral cortex.

This loss of control reduces our reasoning skills and capacity for listening to others.

The above strategy helps a person to return to an emotional state where they have more access to their mental faculties.

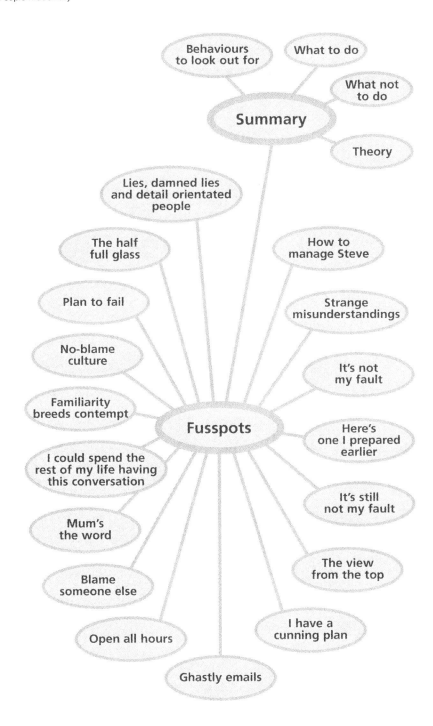

CHAPTER TWO

Fusspots

Understanding detail-orientated people

I was asked to go and see Anne, a senior manager, who was having trouble with a chap called Steve who worked for her. She looked severely harassed. Anne was a tall woman dressed in tweedy, country-style clothes that had seen better days. I asked her to tell me what the problem was. She sighed, leaned back and brushed her hair out of her eyes.

'I just don't know what to do with Steve,' she said. 'It's driving me completely mad. He never seems to do anything I ask him to do. We've got the year-end coming up in a couple of weeks, and because of the recent relocation of the function to Belgium it involves even more work than usual this time.'

I asked her to give me an example of the problem she'd had with Steve.

'Last Thursday morning I came in, and as I passed his desk I said to him: 'Have you phoned Paris yet?' and he just smiled at me and said: "No." So, I went into my office.'

'What happened next?' I asked.

'Half an hour later I came out again and asked him: "Do Paris know about the upgrade yet?" He said: "No." So, I went back into my office. I came out again for some coffee, probably about half past ten, and said to Steve: "Have you told Paris about the upgrade yet?" Again, he said: "No." Then I had a meeting so I was tied up for about half an hour,' Anne said.

'What did you do then?' I asked.

'At the end of the meeting I asked Steve again if he'd phoned Paris. He hadn't. At about quarter to twelve I came out of my office and said to Steve: "The whole system is being shut down at half past twelve today.

Paris must implement the new upgrade before that happens. Phone them and make sure that it's done before the system is shut down." I was furious. Why did I have to ask him five times before he did anything? No one else behaves like that in this office.'

I was beginning to get the picture. But I needed more evidence before I gave Anne any suggestions.

'What about written instructions?' I asked. 'Do you have any emails, for example?'

Anne went to her computer. She explained how she had had terrible trouble getting Steve to do things by email as well. I asked Anne to print out some of the emails and we went through them. She separated them out into a pile of requests that had been completed and ones that had not been completed. The second pile was much the larger. As I looked at the uncompleted emails I felt a sudden stab of recognition. It went through my heart like an ice-cold blade. I realised I was having exactly the same problem in my very own office, with one of my employees. I resolved to check through my own relevant emails when I got back.

The next thing I did was to have a meeting with Steve. Anne took me out into the main office. It was light and airy with a few artificial plants dotted around. She introduced me to Steve. I saw a thin pale man with a large nose and glassy smile. Steve offered me a coffee and then we went into a windowless grey room where a number of chairs surrounded a small wobbly table.

'I understand there have been a few problems in communication between you and your manager,' I said. Steve returned to the glassy smile. I tried again. 'How do you get on with the rest of the team?'

'They leave me out of the loop,' he said.

'Can you give me an example?'

Steve gave me the glassy smile again and said: 'Yes.'

'Tell me what happened,' I asked.

'A few weeks ago some new cost codes were introduced and I needed to know them for part of my work. An email was sent round and I wasn't on the circulation list. So, because of that, I wasn't able to do my job properly.'

'What did you do about it?' I asked. Steve's face smiled, but there was nobody at home. So, I asked again.

'I had to ask Michael for the new codes,' he said.

'What did you do to make sure that you are on the circulation list ready for next time?' I asked.

'I shouldn't have to our ask someone twice to do the same thing,' he told me in tones of great indignation.

I was completely astonished and could not resist asking him about the incident with Anne the previous Thursday.

'Do you remember Anne asking you to phone Paris last Thursday?' I asked.

'Yes.'

'What happened?' I asked eagerly. It's always good to hear the same story told by two different participants. I was itching to hear Steve's side.

Steve went on to tell me what happened. His story was almost the same as Anne's. He recounted exactly how Anne had asked him.

He described how Anne had stopped at his desk when she arrived in the office and asked him if he had phoned Paris yet. He had told her he hadn't. He said that she'd asked him again later whether they knew about the upgrade and then asked him again when she went to get a coffee. He told me how she'd asked him yet again after her meeting. Then at about quarter to twelve she'd told him that Paris had to implement the new upgrade before the system shutdown and that he'd phoned them shortly afterwards. I could detect no concern or guilt at all on his face.

'Steve, you've just told me that you shouldn't have to ask someone twice to do the same thing, but Anne had to ask you five times before you phoned Paris. Why did she have to do that?'

'I don't see why I should have to change my own plan, a plan that I've worked out really carefully, just because my manager said so,' he said while I sat there completely aghast.

At the end of our session, Steve complained to me that our session wasn't what he had been expecting. He said he was expecting some proper training. I asked him if he was able to use the telephone. He said he was. I asked him if he was able to use the English language. He agreed that he was.

'So what training do you need?' I asked. 'Just pick up the phone and tell them to put you on the circulation list.'

This may seem very blunt. It is deliberately so. What have you learnt about Steve so far? One thing that shouts out at you is that he can't take a hint. This means that if you want him to do something you have to be very direct. This would seem rude to many people, but Steve is not *many people*.

When I sat down with Anne she looked troubled and weary. I told her not to worry and said that there was plenty she could do to improve matters. The key was always to give Steve a deadline whenever she asked him to do something. To my surprise she looked concerned and protested that she couldn't really do that because it would be very patronising. She had just come back from an exhaustive management training course – and one of the key principles on the course was trust. She felt that treating Steve in this way would show that she didn't trust him, and that her behaviour would be entirely inappropriate. Of course, for most people it would have been.

This is one of the key problems when you're dealing with any *difficult* person. You imagine he sees the world just as you do, and that he understands the same things and interprets the evidence of his ears and eyes in the same way you do. So you treat him as though this is the case. It doesn't work.

The key is to understand his world and treat him in a way that makes sense to him. It's like being in a foreign country. We have all watched while one English person shouts English loudly at a French person who, quite clearly, doesn't understand. Extre volume doesn't work. You just have to speak French.

How to manage Steve

Let's look at the key evidence surrounding Steve's behaviour. First we will look at the Thursday morning incident. Anne said that she had to ask Steve five times to get him to phone Paris. Why was this? And why did Steve not think his inaction was a problem? Let's look at the five requests:

1 'Have you phoned Paris yet?'

2 'Do Paris know about the upgrade yet?'

3 'Have you told Paris about the upgrade yet?'

4 I again asked Steve if he'd phoned Paris.

5 'The whole system is being shut down at half past twelve today. Paris must implement the new upgrade before that happens. Phone them and make sure that it's done before the system is shut down.'

Let's look at the last sentence. It's different from the others in that it mentions a specific time. This is very important. For most people when they hear something like 'does Paris know about the upgrade yet?' they immediately put it into a global context. They will make the correct assumptions about the urgency (as implied by the tone of voice) and relate it to the situation. Then they will realise (if it's applicable to them) that they need to take some action.

Unfortunately this is not true for people like Steve. In his case, what he does is to look at the sentence in a very detail-orientated and literal way. Steve's answer is grammatically correct. But it's rather like the advice given to the man who lands his balloon in a field and doesn't know where he is:

The man asks a passer-by the question: 'Where am I?'

The passer-by replies: 'You are in any cornfield twenty yards from the gate and three feet from the hedge.'

The balloon pilot responds: 'You must be an accountant.'

The accountant is flabbergasted. 'How did you know that?'

The pilot answers: 'Because everything you've told me is completely accurate but totally useless.'

Steve is a very detail-orientated individual with little ability to take the overview. To understand the context of any incident or request the overview is essential.

Imagine you were only able to view the world through one end of a long tube, rather like the ones that you get inside roles of wrapping paper. Let's say I asked you to find your way from your office to my car, which was parked in a car park some distance away. I might tell you the name of the car park and that my car is a dark grey rather old Audi. How would you do it? At the very least it would be quite difficult to track down my car, because you would not be able to see the overview. As you encounter each obstacle it is very hard to find a way around it.

Assuming you really did have to find my Audi in the car park, as I described it, I would need to give you very detailed step-by-step instructions on how to get from your office to my car. In some ways this is what it's like to be Steve. He does not connect separate events and can't understand the context of a statement – to him it's in isolation. Urgency is something people like Steve seem to find incomprehensible, or perhaps it's fairer to say that they don't notice it.

Let's imagine that you and I were in a meeting together and I said to you: 'I need to visit the bathroom and *urgently*.'

Now let's imagine a telephone conversation. You and I are in separate cities – perhaps even in different countries – and I say to you: 'We need to meet up *urgently*.'

In the first sentence *urgently* probably means *in the next two minutes*. In the second sentence *urgently* may mean *in the next three days* or, depending on the context, *in the next two weeks*.

You understand the meaning of this because you are in the situation and you are familiar with the context. Whereas, if you'd just heard the word on its own, or the sentence on its own, it would be much harder for you to interpret the meaning correctly.

Words and phrases like *immediately, straight away, at once* and *ASAP* are very contextual. For a person who can't see the context, they are either meaningless or open to misinterpretation. To avoid this misinterpretation, and make sure that a person like this understands exactly what you mean, you need to give specific deadlines.

When I got back to Anne's office I went through the details of my meeting with Steve. We checked through other situations. Sure enough only requests that had been accompanied with a deadline had been completed. Not one of the others had been achieved.

'Have you ever had any strange misunderstandings with Steve?' I asked.

She looked surprised. 'Yes, I have. It happens quite often.'

'Does it ever happen with anyone else? I asked.

'No,' she said.

'Anne, it's not you,' I assured her.

'So, Nancy, how did you know about these misunderstandings?' she asked. And I explained by telling her a story about Julie and Kevin:

Strange misunderstandings

Strange misunderstandings like this seem to be common with people who are very detail-orientated and cannot take an overview. It all goes back to our long cardboard tube. When you have a conversation with someone else, what do you remember from it? Is your version always exactly the same as his or hers? Probably not, but usually you will have the gist of it right. The problem occurs when you remember the gist of the conversation and the other person remembers one specific sentence. Let's take an example.

I worked with Julie on a problem she had with one of her project managers. Julie was an experienced manager, a woman who dressed more for comfort than for speed. She had a kindly, if slightly worried, face.

'I spent half an hour with Kevin explaining the project,' she said. 'I asked him to complete a plan for it. I also suggested that Kevin phone a colleague, Mark, about an aspect of that project. Two weeks later when I expected Kevin to give me the plan nothing arrived. The following week I went to see Kevin and asked him where the plan was. He seemed confused. When I explained that I was referring to the conversation of a few weeks ago Kevin told me he had phoned Mark and he hadn't been there.'

'I couldn't understand what was going on and asked Kevin why he hadn't tried phoning Mark again,' Julie continued.

'What was Kevin's response?' I asked.

'He just looked confused and said to me that I had told him to phone Mark.'

What had happened here was that Kevin remembered one small part of the conversation and, in his view, had followed the instructions to the letter. Julie, his manager, could not understand why Kevin, at the very least, had not come back to her and admitted he was having problems. The reason for this is that he was completely unaware of the context. And the manager had not suggested that if Mark were out then he should try and call him again later.

Let's go back to Steve and Anne. Remember, Anne had asked Steve five times to complete the same task; phoning Paris to tell them about a computer upgrade. My suggestion to Anne was that she gave Steve very clear deadlines for every piece of work she asked him to complete and that she also showed him an overview of the situation. She already had a plan printed out in a table, which included everyone in the team and showed each of their required actions. I suggested she gave Steve a copy of this with his specific tasks highlighted. She still felt this was a little patronising but agreed to try it.

Let's look back at the last request Anne made to Steve about phoning Paris, when she also told him about the time deadline. Notice how Anne also told Steve exactly what she wanted him to do: *'The whole system is being shut down at half past twelve today. Paris must implement the new upgrade before that happens. Phone them and make sure that it's done before the system is shut down.'*

Her other requests were just requests for information. Steve complied with all of them; he just didn't look at the whole context and work out what Anne really meant.

When I went back to see Anne two weeks later she was looking much happier. She had on a smart navy suit and a broad smile. She was very pleased to tell me that Steve had completed all that she had given him on time. She told me her meeting with him had taken a little longer than usual. Anne had explained exactly what she wanted Steve to do. She had explained each step to him and showed him where he fitted into the overall plan. Nevertheless the amount of time she'd had to spend chasing him up had been drastically reduced. Anne felt this was a good result.

The results were impressive but Anne still felt guilty about having to manage Steve in this way. We discussed it.

'Anne, would you feel guilty about helping someone in a wheelchair to take the lift to the top floor?' I asked.

'Not at all,' she said. Anne had a disabled member of staff in her team and everyone helped him quite happily.

'This is just the same. You are helping Steve to do something that he can't do. He may improve in time, but at the moment, it's not possible for him.'

It's not my fault

Let's look at another aspect of Steve's behaviour. This involves his lack of responsibility. Do you remember Steve complained about being 'left out of the loop'? When I asked him what he was going to do to make sure he was included in the circulation list next time, he told me that he shouldn't have to ask someone twice to do the same thing.

This approach is in complete contrast to his manager's approach. She was desperate for anything she could do that would change things. She had taken complete responsibility for the situation. Steve, on the other hand, did not think he bore any responsibility at all for what was happening. Once you start to think like that it becomes very difficult to affect a situation. He felt he needed some kind of 'training' when all he needed to do was to pick up the phone and speak to the person responsible for the circulation list.

This kind of thought pattern can cause many problems because it means that people don't take action when you would normally expect them to.

Here's one I prepared earlier

The first thing to remember is that when these things happen, it's not always your fault. You just have to alter your style to suit the person you are working with. All requests must be given as a list of instructions with clear times and deadlines. Never assume that the person will work it out for himself. He just does not have access to the information that will enable him to do that.

On a training course I was running, one of the team leaders, Nicola, brought up a problem. Nicola was young and keen with bright green eyes and sandy hair. She looked very fit and sporty to me. Her example was a fascinating one – a person with exactly this detail-orientated behaviour.

Bernadette was very good at her job as long as nothing changed and nothing unexpected happened. Her job was to carry out tests on various samples. In fact she carried out hundreds of the same test each day. Bernadette was known to be extremely accurate and reliable. She was a bird-like woman in her fifties, with straight mousy hair and very neat in her appearance. Her clothes were always perfectly ironed and spotless.

Nicola gave us some astonishing background information about Bernadette. She told us that, at home, this woman had all the meals for the next month ready prepared and in her freezer on plates. I spent some time imagining how that would work. Were the plates china or paper? Did she have an upright freezer or chest freezer? And how did she rotate the stock? I had little doubt that she had a very strict regime in place.

This piece of background information gave a useful insight into Bernadette's character. Here was a person who loved following procedures and whose life was organised well in advance. This is completely different from making a large pot of stew and putting the leftovers in the freezer at the end of the meal.

The problem for Nicola was that when the equipment Bernadette was working on broke down, or someone else needed to use it in a hurry, Bernadette panicked. I suggested to Nicola that she wrote out a procedure for these specific situations with a list (preferably numbered) of the actions that she had to take.

I suggested something like:

1 When the equipment breaks down switch it off.

2 Remove your sample.

3 Phone the engineer.

4 Or ask your manager what he would like you to do.

Everyone thought this was hilarious until Nicola came back on the next module of the course and told us all that this strategy had worked very well.

The reason this worked so well is that Bernadette now had a set of instructions telling her exactly what to do in all the difficult situations. She had simply been unable to take a step back and work out for herself what she needed to do.

It's still not my fault

I worked with a manager, Ramzan, who had inherited two *poor performers*. He was talking about how he expected them to be more responsible and was planning to tell them that they had to take responsibility for some things.

In a situation like this it is vital to make sure that the person really knows what you mean by *taking responsibility*. One of the *poor performers,* Joanne, was going to be work-shadowing a colleague. I suggested to Ramzan that he explained in detail what he expected Joanne to do in that situation. We went through the key tasks involved:

1 The first task was that when Joanne did not understand something, she was to say: 'I don't understand' and then ask for help.

2 The second was that at the beginning of the week Joanne was to make her objectives clear to the manager she was shadowing. This meant that she needed to explain to him exactly what she wanted to learn by shadowing him.

3 Finally, halfway through the week Joanne was to review what she had learned and what she had not learned. Once she had identified what she still needed, she had to explain this to her manager.

Ramzan explained this to Joanne with the result that the work shadowing was far more successful than he had anticipated. Just as an experiment, he told the second *poor performer*, Eric, to take responsibility but did not explain to him what it meant. His work shadowing was not a successful experience.

The view from the top

One of my clients, June, told me she'd had tremendous difficulties getting one of her employees to plan ahead. The staff member, Angela, had wanted to take on a large project. Against her better judgement, June had agreed that Angela could take it on as a development activity. Unfortunately, this major project was pivotal to the success of the department. June knew she was taking a risk but felt strongly that people should have the opportunity to develop.

June decided to monitor Angela's progress carefully. Two weeks after agreeing that Angela should take on the project she asked to see Angela's plan. Angela said she couldn't show it to her. June asked why not. Angela told her that it wasn't really in a form suitable for viewing. June asked when it would be and Angela was reluctant to say. June told her she wanted to see something by the end of the following week. Then she felt a little guilty because she realised that Angela had not managed anything like this before. She asked Angela if she needed some help and sent her a copy of some project management software.

After another week there was still no plan. June decided to pay a visit to Angela's office and see what was going on. She asked Angela to show her the plan as it stood. To her astonishment Angela retrieved several very large pieces of paper with tiny words written in pencil on them in what seemed to be no particular order.

People who are very detail-orientated find it hard to plan. This is because planning involves taking an overview. A key aspect of planning is prioritisation. In order to prioritise you need to step back, take the overview and identify which tasks have priority. Looking at a project through a long cardboard tube makes prioritisation virtually impossible.

June asked me for some help. When you are coaching someone who has some difficult behaviours, it is very important to be clear about your objectives. You must agree exactly what you want to be different, once the coaching is finished.

As a trainer and coach with many years' experience, I am completely convinced that you can train almost anyone to do almost anything. But before you start you need to ask yourself two questions: Do I have the budget? And will they live that long? My experience with this particular problem is that although you can help a person to improve his or her flexibility to a certain extent, it seems to be very difficult in some cases to really help them make a lot of progress. However we decided to give it to try.

I have a cunning plan

One of the key aspects of planning, as we discussed earlier, is the ability to take the overview. Fortunately, this is a skill that can be learned. The key is to get someone to start seeing the 'big picture' in some part of his life. To start with, this can be any area of his life; the context does not have to be related to what you are working on with him.

One of the most successful examples of this was Alan. He was having terrible problems with a big software project. He found himself constantly dragged into the detail and focusing on small, not very significant, problems. During our first session he spent almost half an hour telling me about one of them. I asked him to draw it on a piece of paper. To him it seemed like a tangled ball of wool. I took the piece of paper and put it on the floor. I then asked him to stand on a chair and look at it. As he did so his face lit up and he said to me: 'It's really not that big a problem, is it?'

Alan was about to go on holiday. As part of his homework, I suggested that he buy three maps, each on a different scale. Everywhere he went, he was to look at each of the maps. The idea of this was to get his brain used to getting into detail and coming out to get a look at the big picture.

As a result of our work together, Alan managed to find himself a new job doing exactly what he wanted to do, which was managing large projects. Alan worked very hard at learning these skills and was very keen to improve. It's always much easier working with someone who wants to improve, and who can see the value of it. Sometimes a person is so detail-orientated that I wonder whether he has any idea at all of the entire big picture.

I was concerned that this was the problem here with Angela. To start with, I spent quite some time drawing diagrams for her that I hoped would give her an idea of the big picture in various different situations. Then we both read the same book. I asked her to give me a summary of it. She found the task almost impossible. She had no idea where to start. Not knowing where to start means you have a problem with prioritisation. I produced a mind map TM of the book and sent it to her.

The diagrams at the beginning of this book and at the beginning of each chapter are mind maps.

Angela was completely stunned by the mind map I had drawn of the book. But because I had forgotten to give her a date by which she was to come back to me about her thoughts, several weeks went by before we spoke about it. Angela told me she could never have produced the map. I asked her why not and she told me that she wouldn't know where to start. Even when I gave a step-by-step guide she still had difficulties and most of them were to do with prioritisation.

Although Angela did make some progress, the main benefits came from managing her a different way. This meant that June always had to put everything in context for Angela, and she had to give clear step-by-step instructions when she wanted her to do anything. Whenever she forgot to do that, or just assumed that it was obvious, there were problems.

During her summer holidays, June had come across a puzzle that she thought would make a nice Christmas present for some of her clients. She examined the box, and, although there was a supplier's name, there was no phone number, address or website. June described the puzzle to Angela and explained how she thought it would make a good present for some of their clients. She gave Angela the details she had, expecting her to take some action.

After several weeks she had heard nothing. In the end she searched the web herself and found a website under construction. Fortunately it gave the name of the town where the company was located. So she called Directory Inquiries, got the phone number and gave them a ring.

It turned out that she had called just in time. The manager told her that he was just completing his large orders for his stockists in time for Christmas, and had very few puzzles left. June ordered enough for her customers.

Several months later (two weeks before Christmas) June had an email from Angela saying that she had searched the Internet and found the web site giving the details of the puzzle supplier. She gave the web address in the email. That was all she had done. Angela had completely missed the point. She had not been able to prioritise correctly, or understand the context of the conversation. She had no idea that June expected her to track down the company, and, at the very least, get some ordering details, such as price and lead time in time for Christmas.

Let's consider why this may have happened.

Earlier in the chapter we discussed Steve. As you'll remember, he worked for Anne. She had had major problems getting him to do things. We had looked at a number of emails she'd sent him, and discovered that only the tasks where he had been given a deadline had been completed.

Steve didn't see why he should change his personal plan just for Anne, even if she was his manager. It seems that Angela was doing the same thing. In fact, what they were both doing was putting any new task they were given to the end of their list.

These people tend to have one long list for all their tasks. No matter how important, urgent or vital the task is, the procedure they use is simply to put any new task at the end of the list unless a clear time constraint is added.

It was only by chance that Angela had investigated the puzzles before Christmas at all.

Ghastly emails

I was working with an American client who told me he was having severe problems with one of his managers. George was a large character. He must have been well over six feet tall and always reminded me of Yogi Bear.

George looked calm. His great bear-eyes peered at me with a mournful look. 'I keep getting these emails from Manjit,' he said.

He opened up his laptop and clicked on an email. It was very long. Here's just the beginning:

> **Dear George**
>
> I have been very upset recently by the way you have been
> ignoring me and deliberately not keeping me up to date with
> the progress on the DELILA project. Over the last three months I
> have worked very hard under very difficult circumstances on
> this project. I have stayed until 7pm every night for the last
> three weeks and on three occasions I worked until 10pm. You
> don't seem to realise how much effort I have put in on this
> project and I am very disappointed that you do not appreciate
> all my hard work. I have hardly seen my family and they too
> have made sacrifices to ensure that DELILA gets off the ground.
>
> When we talked a week ago last Wednesday all you said
> was that you were 'disappointed with the progress'. I find
> this a very hurtful remark.

The email started off by telling George, my client, how are upset she, Manjit, was about the situation. It went on to describe how hard she worked, listing out the numbers of hours that had been put in on various days. It continued with a harrowing account of how George clearly did not value Manjit, how all her efforts went unappreciated, and how George never supported her and should help out more.

He clicked on another email, also from Manjit. The second was almost as long and just as accusatory as the first. From the emails I got the impression that George didn't care, worked his people to death and took no interest whatsoever in their work. Fortunately I knew George well enough to know this was untrue. So how was it that Manjit had managed to get this impression?

Perhaps you remember the section earlier, on strange misunderstandings. We discussed what it's like looking at the world through a long cardboard tube and how easy it can be for a very detail-orientated person to focus on one specific thing and not notice the context. Manjit's situation is an extension of that one.

In this case Manjit had got stuck on one particular problem, which had caused her to feel quite stressed. For most of us, when we feel stressed we tend to focus more on detail. There are some very sensible reasons for this and if you are familiar with the 'fight or flight' response you will immediately recognise these symptoms. When you are threatened you get an adrenaline response. This is designed to help you survive the next five or ten minutes. What your body does is shut down any non-essential functions so that all your energy can be refocused on your survival. These non-essential functions include your digestive system, repair mechanisms, your immune system, reproduction and, among other things, your ability to think long term.

Why is this? Well if you are about to be run over by a bus, planning your pension is not going to help you a great deal. Nor is digesting your lunch. Long-term thinking, goal setting and planning activities tend to take place in the frontal lobes of your brain. These activities are all redundant for very short-term survival. Running away may be a much more useful activity. So, very sensibly, your body channels all the energy that would have been put wasted on these other activities into running away (or fighting).

Unfortunately this happens whether the threat involves something physical or not. So for Manjit, although the situation did not involve a physical threat, her body's response was just the same. We just tend to call it stress these days.

For a person who is already detail-orientated, this means that he becomes focused on a very small area and is not *able* to see anything else. So if he has encountered a problem (and that's usually the case when he feels stressed) his whole mind and consciousness will be focused on that problem. It will take up all his awareness. What he will tend to do is extrapolate the problem until it becomes an entire universe. Everyone's behaviour will be interpreted in the light of this problem. So if we look at Manjit's email, we notice two specific interesting features.

One is the emphasis on the hard work and long hours; the other is the emphasis on blaming someone else. We will address the long hours first.

Open all hours

This behaviour is often a warning sign that you have a detail-orientated person with little ability to take the overview. The reason behind the long hours and hard work is the belief that achieving more must always be down to working harder. They do not have an awareness of *working smarter*. This is because *working smarter* involves taking an overview. You have to stand back, look at the situation, see new connections and find new ways of doing things before you can *work smarter.*

When you manage a person with this way of looking at the world, every time you ask him to do something else, or to achieve more, he automatically assumes it means he must work harder and for longer hours. You, on the other hand, may find taking the overview easy, so you have no trouble at all spotting shortcuts and quick ways of achieving various tasks. In fact you may be astonished at the lengthy methods this person uses for achieving his objectives.

So, when you ask your detail-orientated person to do something, it is very hard to judge how much effort he is going to be putting in. This is because you probably know efficient, easy, ways of carrying out the task yourself, so you assume (if you think about it at all) that he will take the easy way too. The detail-orientated person is often unaware of these quick ways, so works really hard and for long hours, believing that hard, long hours are, *in themselves,* valuable.

Here's an example of how it works. On one Time Management course I ran, several of the participants complained about a meeting they had attended recently. The meeting was in a department of some hundred and fifty people, and scheduled for 3-4pm. Of the five people on my Time Management course, who had attended that meeting, three had young children. The children were cared for at various local nurseries. These nurseries always have a deadline by which time you have to have picked your children. In this case, all the nurseries had a deadline of 6pm (which all the participants felt was quite reasonable).

The director who was running the meeting had something of a reputation for his love of detail. The meeting over-ran (due to his poor skill levels in this area) and was still going at 5.30pm, one and a half hours after its published finish time. When the people with children to collect got up to leave, the director made all kinds of unpleasant comments about people not being committed to the company and not working hard enough. In his view, they should have stayed at the meeting. He was unable to understand that, having been given a finish time of 4pm, they had made arrangements around that. They'd had (so they thought) plenty of margin for error – one and a half hours – but that had been completely used up.

The director was only able to judge people's value to the organisation in terms of the hours they put in, rather than the results they achieved. In his universe, he was staying late, so they should too, or else they were not committed. This shows a very narrow view of the world and an inability to understand the circumstances of others. Often this stems from a very detail-orientated view of the world. The others who had been at the meeting, those without children, said they too had felt acutely embarrassed by the director's remarks.

Going back to George and Manjit – it seemed to Manjit that her efforts were not valued. In fact, she was correct in this. George valued the results that were achieved, not the amount of effort put in due to ineffective working practices. Manjit did not understand this concept. She had once commented to George, in quite an aggressive manner, that she did not like performance-based pay. She thought it unfair. This is because, in her eyes, those who work the hardest and longest should be paid the most (conveniently for her). Unfortunately, paying those who work the longest hours the most money can encourage people to work long hours rather than find more effective ways of achieving their goals.

Blame someone else

The second feature in the email Manjit sent is the element of blame. It was clear that Manjit felt all the blame lay on George's shoulders. She had worked like a slave in order to achieve all the tasks he had set her – but he had not appreciated her efforts. How does this happen? It happens because the person's focus is directed to him or herself. When you focus mainly on detail and do not take the overview, that detail is bound to be very close to you, or where you are. Almost always, it involves you.

If you believe you have done everything possible in the situation and worked tremendously hard, then it follows logically for most people that you can't be at fault. Obviously it must be the fault of the other person for having given you too much work to do.

You know you have worked your socks off; no one could have worked harder. And that is probably true. No one could have worked harder. The sad part is: no one else *would* have worked that hard. Everyone else would have found a much easier way of achieving the task. And your manager has assumed that you too would find an easy way.

As the manager, how can you effectively manage such a situation? The first thing is that you must keep a close eye on what the person is actually doing – not what you think he is doing or have assumed he is doing. Before you let this person go off and do a task, you need to check how long he thinks it will take. And if it's longer than you think is reasonable you need to find out how he's planning to achieve that task.

Of course, I am making this sound very easy and I have conveniently ignored another problem that you may encounter.

Mum's the word

I have seen this problem occur on several occasions. The manager gives a task to his detail-orientated team member and the team member works long and hard, much harder than anyone else, to achieve it. Then the manager wonders why. As a concerned individual, the manager tries to find out what happened – and is flabbergasted to be accused of not trusting his team member. The manager finds himself being asked why he needs that information, and the harder he tries to find out what is happening the worse it gets. So he gives up. Interestingly, this combination can quite easily lead to bullying. Here's how:

The detail-orientated person feels he is not being trusted because he is asked questions that he misinterprets. He misinterprets them because he can't see the overall picture. So he assumes they are attacks and starts to behave defensively.

The only way for the detail-orientated person (in his view) to please the manager is to work harder and longer hours. So he feels victimised because he is working so hard and for so many hours. He complains about how hard he is working and talks about all the hours he is putting in. Unfortunately, because he is not achieving very much, his manager sees this as moaning and becomes annoyed. This then may encourage an aggressive response in the manager. This can then look like bullying to the detail-orientated person. For at least one of the cases of bullying I have worked on, detail orientation has been shown to be a contributory factor. We discuss bullying in another chapter.

What, then, can you do in a situation like this? Well, you need to work more closely with the individual and start to understand things from his point of view. The detail-orientated person then needs to know that you value his contribution and that you are trying to help him. When you talk with him, you need to listen and summarise what he's said back to him, to show him that you have been listening. People who have these traits seem to need a lot of attention and feedback in order to know how well they are doing.

For example:

'Why did that take so long?' The question phrased this way is almost bound to cause hard feeling because it can be interpreted as a threat. So what tends to happen when you use this approach is that the person feels even more threatened and thus more stressed. He then becomes even more detail-orientated – and on the cycle goes.

Here is another way to address the problem:

'I realise you have been working very hard on this problem recently. You've put a great deal of time and effort into it. I didn't realise there was so much involved in the task.' At this point you will probably get at least some murmurings from him and may even get the whole story. If not, you have now shown yourself to be an understanding manager. You have some options open to you.

You could continue with something like:

'What can I do to help?' or
'Tell me what you've managed to do so far.'

As the person starts to talk, it is very important that you continually comment on how hard he is working and how much you appreciate all his efforts. Otherwise you will end up in the situation we talked about earlier, where he will think you are a hard taskmaster deliberately working your people into an early grave.

The key in dealing with this situation is to remember that the detail-orientated person has a very tiny fragment of information and is building his whole world based on that fragment. By gradually giving him some other information, you make it easier for him to build a more accurate picture of the situation. Where possible, I recommend very strongly that you show him some kind of diagram or picture illustrating exactly where his tasks fit in, and how he fits into whatever it is you are doing. This can be a stunning insight for a detail-orientated person and also reduces his stress levels quite considerably.

By keeping this up consistently, it can help him to develop the skill of taking an overview himself, which would be a wonderful long term benefit for both of you.

Remember, this behaviour is not in any way deliberate. In my experience, people don't go out of their way to do things the hard way. They do the best they are able to in the circumstances. You need to change those circumstances – but in a way that makes sense to the person concerned. It's no good telling someone to find an easy way if he doesn't know how to do that. He will usually need some kind of procedure. That means you need to give a list of instructions. It could be as simple as:

1 Saying: *'Please find ten different models of photocopier that cost under two hundred pounds by the end of next week.'*

2 Drawing up a table to show which models have which functions.

3 Saying: *'Let me know how far you've got with this task on Friday.'* At this point it might be useful to ask the person how long he thinks it's going to take, although usually he will find it quite difficult to answer that question.

Notice that I have suggested you ask for an update on 'Friday'. This is so that you can check how he is doing the task and to make sure he'll do it in a relatively easy way.

I could spend the rest of my life having this conversation

Manjit's emails to George were very long; his replies were short. Their conversations were similar each time. This is quite a common pattern when a globally-orientated person is talking with a detail-orientated person.

When I recruited our bookkeeper I was looking for a detail-orientated person. I knew that this meant he or she would probably give answers three or four times longer that I would. One of my key measures for the detail-orientated behaviour I was looking for was the length of the interview. The first interview was over in ten minutes. This was not the person I was looking for. We needed someone who enjoyed the detail and therefore would give me detail in his or her answer to each question.

The successful candidate's initial interview took half an hour (the questions were almost identical to those for the ten minute interview). She is still with us, and she still keeps a close eye on all the detail.

Here's the kind of thing I mean:

Me:	*'Where did you gain most of your bookkeeping experience?'*
Unsuccessful candidate:	*'At my first company.'*
Me:	*'Where did you gain most of your bookkeeping experience?'*
Successful candidate:	*'When I first worked for Henderson's, I was in a small accounts department and they paid for me to go on a course. I did quite a bit of bookkeeping for them there. Then I moved to another site on the other side of the town and started on the books there. They were in a terrible mess and it took me a while to sort them out, but I learned a lot.'*

One of the problems for the less detail-orientated person is that, the more detail they are given, the less they give – so the conversations become increasingly one-sided. The detail-orientated person gives an answer of two paragraphs and the globally orientated person gives one-word answers. They tend to make each other worse.

The global person gets bored, wants to end the conversation quickly, and wants shorter responses; as a result they give shorter and shorter responses. The detail-orientated person feels that the global person does not understand the detail and is not listening (he is probably right) so he gives *more* detail. The conversation can spin out of control with both parties getting very frustrated. The answer is for each to adapt a little to the other's style.

Whenever you find yourself giving very short answers to someone's long and detailed answers, consciously make your answers lengthier. Summarise what they have said to show you are listening as well, and you will often find their responses become shorter. This seems completely counter-intuitive, but it does work. Try it.

Familiarity breeds contempt

I was discussing with a client where he should put one of his staff who was very detail-orientated. We had already agreed he should be moved from his current position.

'But of course, he will get on with others who're like him, so perhaps we should put him with some similar people and he'd be happier,' he suggested.

It was a mistake I had made myself. Sadly it doesn't work. If you are in a very small box and are introduced to someone else in a very small box a few miles away, how will either of you be able to understand how your boxes are linked without the ability to take an overview? Seeing the other person's point of view would be very difficult.

Detail-orientated people have their own, detailed view, of a very small part of the world. They often have firm beliefs on how it works and how things should be done in that part of the world. They are usually completely unaware of other's views. So if you put two very detail-orientated people together they are quite likely to have greatly differing views on many things.

Astonishingly, when I have worked with people like this, several of them reserved their most severe criticisms for those who were most similar to themselves.

Simon, a very detail-orientated person I coached, spent almost a whole session criticising a customer who was always moaning about problems and never seemed to have any answers. Simon dealt with many customers and was fastidious in both his appearance and his form-filling. He hated people who couldn't fill in forms correctly (I omitted to confess this as one of my own faults). Simon's behaviour seemed identical to the customer's but he was oblivious to this until I pointed it out. Even then, in his mind, his behaviour was more justifiable than the customer's, and he found it hard to look at things from the customer's point of view.

Sam, one of the most detail-orientated people I have ever worked with, told me she needed to attend a project meeting. Sam wore thin, schoolteacher glasses and a constant frown. Even when she was smiling she frowned. I once asked her if she was all right because I thought she looked worried and she insisted (with a frown) that she was enjoying herself. At the same time she told me about a colleague of hers. Sam remarked that Jenny shouldn't be at the meeting because she wasn't a global person and was far too detail-orientated.

I could hardly believe my ears because, personally, I had thought the meeting would be inappropriate for Sam for exactly the same reason. Jenny, in my view, had a much better handle on the overall situation.

Jenny was a quiet, careful, individual, but had a ready wit and quick smile. She often looked a little nervous but soon warmed up.

I happened to chair that very meeting and it was almost a complete failure due to Sam's lack of perspective. She got stuck on one point. Her frown deepened and she was unable to see that the issue concerning her was irrelevant to the situation. Sam spent much of the meeting telling everyone how the whole project would be impossible – much to the surprise and annoyance of the others involved. They were more familiar than Sam with the technology involved.

Sam glared at us doggedly over her spectacles. She kept on telling us that the project would take up too much time, and that the postage costs would be phenomenal. She had not realised the client had a paperless system. Others tried to explain it to her. She told them they didn't understand, and that a project like the one we were discussing generated tons of paperwork, and we didn't have the staff to deal with it.

In the end I had to take her to one side. By this time she was very upset because she thought we weren't taking the problems seriously and she would be the one having to work long hours because the company was understaffed in that area – and on it went. It was as though her whole mind was shut to any view but her own. The more upset she became, the less she was able to understand.

This happens because, as you become more upset, you become less able to see any positive aspects of anything. Most people also focus more on the detail as they become more upset. When they start off as very detail-orientated, the results can be grisly. In this case I was surprised by the speed of the decline. It was a great mistake to have allowed Sam to come to the meeting in the first place. It would have been far better to explain it all to her later in a way that would have made it easier for her to understand.

No-blame culture

I always feel concerned when someone talks to me about his no blame culture. In my view I prefer to talk about a responsibility culture. How do you deal with the detail-orientated person's view that most problems are someone else's fault?

Firstly, you need to remember that detail-orientated people do not do this on purpose. The reason they think it's someone else's fault is because their focus of attention is so narrow. It is usually based around themselves and what other people think of them. They may well be thinking in a very defensive way if they feel stressed, and so imagine that other people are going to blame them. In order to defend themselves they will point out how hard they have been working. What they will not do is look around and see what else is going on.

An easy way to help someone start thinking about taking responsibility is to ask him whom he thinks is responsible for each element of a given situation. Once you have helped him to establish that, it is often a good idea to identify exactly what you mean by responsibility. For example, if you agree with a person working for you that he is responsible for a task, you may want to also agree that this means he is responsible for planning it too. It is often wise to discuss exactly what you mean by 'planning'.

I am aware that you may think I'm being rather fussy here. Yes, I am. And that's because I have made this mistake many times myself and have seen many of my clients make it too. We have assumed that what we asked for was obvious and, as a result, we've got something completely different from what we expected.

Plan to fail

I worked with Helena, who had previously worked in an organisation where she was told every day exactly what she had to do. She was given a list of tasks, she was told how long each task was likely to take and she was then told to go away and complete them. On numerous occasions she complained to her manager and said she would really like to plan her time out herself. Her manager told her that wasn't really possible because only he knew what everyone needed to do and only he was capable of planning all his or her time.

Helena dressed like a student. I guess I would have appreciated her taste in fashion if I had been younger. She had the kind of hair that stays straight no matter what you do to it and she had tried to tie it back. She wore Nana Mouskouri glasses with heavy black frames but they suited her very well.

She had transferred to another department. The manager of this department had a very different approach, not only to his work, but also to life in general. I knew him quite well. He was very much a happy-go-lucky type, with a cheerful spring in his stride that made him almost bounce along the long corridors of the building where he worked. He always dressed very well and I later discovered that his wife bought all his clothes for him.

Barry liked people to take responsibility, have ideas and plan their own time. He was horrified by the thought of planning in anyone's time for them. When I sat down with his new team member, Helena, in her disorganised office, she told me, in embarrassed tones, that although she had always wanted to plan out her own time she had no idea where to start. That was quite plain with one glance at the desk, which was obscured by a mass of papers, books, writing implements and what looked like old sandwiches (I didn't check too closely). Planning appeared to be a very difficult task for her and she was horrified that, having wanted to do this for so long, when she finally had the opportunity she was completely stuck.

I gave her a few basic suggestions and very quickly she developed the skills. It had never occurred to Barry that anyone could have such a low level of skill in this area. He had not noticed the problems because he had not investigated. He just thought she seemed a little overworked.

The half full glass

Most of the people I have come across, who fall into the category of being very detail-orientated and unable to take an overview, have tended to see the world in negative terms. Given any situation they assume the worst, think that everyone is out to get them and start getting worried about any situation. Very occasionally I've encountered the exact opposite: someone who does not see the problem at all. This is a person who is unbelievably cheerful. I have some friends who own a farm. Joe works on that farm.

Joe is a cheerful, round-faced individual who looks as though his skin has been polished by an expert. He beams with health and heartiness and is friendly and helpful to everyone he meets. Every time we visit our friends they tell us a new Joe story. My favourite is the story about the gate.

Joe was asked to hang a gate in the fence surrounding a field. Joe picked up some tools and set off towards the field about three miles away from the farmhouse. The gate he was replacing lay in the far corner. When he arrived he started working on the hinges, but, after a few minutes, he discovered he could not undo one of the bolts because he did not have his spanner with him. Dropping the tools that were in his hand at the time, he started the three-mile walk back to the farmhouse.

When he got back to the farmhouse, he picked up the spanner and set off again on the three-mile journey to the gate. When he got to the gate he was unable to start work again, because he could not find the screwdriver he had dropped into the long grass before he set off to find the spanner. So he returned once more to the farmhouse to fetch a screwdriver. On returning with the screwdriver he then found he had no hammer. So he had to make a third return journey back to the farmhouse before he could complete his task. When my friend went to inspect the gate he noticed a problem.

'There are two ways to hang a gate in the field that lies on the side of a hill. You can hang the gate so that it swings open into the field on the downward slope or so that it swings open into the field on the upward slope,' explained my friend. No doubt you have guessed what Joe had not; if you use the second option the gate does not open. The gate did not open.

The interesting thing about Joe is that he is always happy. He has several children, lives on a very low wage and works hard. Most of us would not class him as lucky. And yet it would be hard to find a happier man. The reason is that he is so focused on the present moment that he simply has nothing to worry about. I will be looking at very negatively orientated people later on, and identify why they see the world as such an unpleasant and unhappy place. For Joe, whose forward planning looks as far ahead as the next two or three minutes, there are very few problems in the world.

When you think about it, for most of the time, you are reasonably happy and comfortable. Much of your stress comes from worrying about things that never happen. I heard some statistics suggesting that eighty per cent of the events we worry about never happen. So eighty per cent of our worrying is a waste of time. Joe doesn't do that and saves himself a lot of grief.

My friend, who owns the farm, said to me one day that he has a beautiful estate set in a lovely part of the country, owns many properties and is what most people would call wealthy. But he spends much of his time worrying about the future, the problems in the industry, his tax bill and disasters that might befall his estate. He will never be as happy as Joe.

Lies, damned lies and detail-orientated people

Mary, a client of mine in an advertising agency, recounted a situation she had witnessed. Unusually for someone in advertising, she is very quiet and retiring. Her clothes seem to merge with the background whenever possible. She related how her colleague, Dave (much more the normal advertising sort: loud in both dress and manner), had spoken on the phone with Tim, a client. He was talking about some packaging they were designing. She heard Dave say quite clearly that the new packaging design should have a black interior.

'John just wasn't listening in the meeting,' Mary heard Dave say. 'Don't worry, Tim, I'll remind John that it must be black. I think you are absolutely right – that is what we agreed in the meeting.'

Not two minutes later, John, the manager, came by. He asked Dave if he had talked with the client, Tim, about the red interior.

Mary told me she wondered what Dave was going to do now – as she'd just heard him assuring the clients that it would be black, while his manager was clear it should be red.

Dave then said: 'They've changed their minds. They want it black now. I told them that's what you said in the first place. They clearly got it wrong.'

Mary had been astonished. She could not understand how Dave could say such a thing, sitting there, knowing she had heard every word.

The truth comes in several layers: Dave did not know that Mary had heard every word and so that was never in his consciousness. As Dave spoke first with the client, Tim, and then with his manager, Brian, all his focus was on each individual conversation. He did not relate the two conversations to each other. They were completely separate entities.

To Mary, the two conversations were clearly part of one whole, so she saw the second conversation as a lie.

Detail-orientated people seem to behave in this way when they are talking to people separately whose views are different. They will agree with each one, even though that means they are being inconsistent in their own views. In order to be consistent, you need to take an overview and link separate events. If you can't do that, then you are unlikely to behave consistently or hold consistent views. Others may see this as lying, but I don't think it is deliberate in these cases.

Summary

Behaviours to look out for

You think you have agreed an action with the person and it does not happen

When you investigate they will have done a very small part of the task, got stuck and gone no further.

Things do not happen when you need them to happen

You will have asked for something to be done, thinking it was obvious that it was really urgent. The person will have left the task for later.

There are strange misunderstandings that only happen with that person, not with anyone else

For example: You will have had queries from this person over one small phrase in an email or letter. Another example might be that this person will remember a conversation you had with him to have had a completely different conclusion to the one you remember.

The person thinks they are very good at planning, but your view is different

His is good at planning in the short term in great detail, but does not seem to think about the longer term at all.

This person cannot see the big picture

He may quibble over tiny amounts of money while not considering the bigger picture. He may have the reputation of being a 'nit-picker'.

He tends to give long answers to your questions

He may tend to continue waffling when you consider the conversation should be over.

He works in a step-by-step manner

He likes to follow a process. When there is no process, he is unhappy or does not know what to do.

There is little or no initiative

When things change, he does not modify his approach accordingly. He rarely comes up with ideas.

What to do

- **Identify whether the person ever does what you ask him to do.** If you can spot situations like this, then ask yourself what the difference might be between these situations and the ones that give you trouble. Once you have the difference, then you usually have a way forward. It may include having things written down and giving clear deadlines, or it may be about giving step-by-step instructions.

- **Always give a deadline.** Although it may seem obvious to you how urgent something is, it is not obvious to him. Words like 'immediately', 'urgent', 'straight away' and 'soon' mean different things to different people.

- **Check his understanding of the context.** Make sure it's the same as yours. A person who is very detail-orientated may not be aware of the context and will therefore not be able to prioritise effectively.

- **Check how stressed the person is.** The more stressed, the more difficult it is for him to prioritise and plan.

- **Give clear priorities.** You need to give him the priorities and also let him know when these change. Don't expect him to 'just know'. You may have to do this on a daily or weekly basis.

- **Ask for his plan whenever you ask him to do something.** This will give you a good indication of his understanding. It may be that your instructions are not clear. We always think we have explained ourselves clearly, but that is not always the case. It will also give you a clue as to whether he is working smart or just working hard.

- **Give long answers to his questions.** You need to communicate using the same level of detail as the other person. If your answers are short and lacking in detail, it appears to this person that you don't know what you are talking about. He will simply start asking for even more detail, or give you more detail still, because he thinks you don't fully understand the situation.

- **Summarise what he has said** rather than just responding 'Yes' or 'No'. This helps him to feel that he has been listened to and will help to reduce his 'waffling'.

  Wrong: *'Yes.'*

Right: *'Yes, I think we should replace the old photocopier. I am glad you have looked at 17 different models and analysed the prices so carefully. I agree that we should go with the Model RTD 1000. It will give us the best deal and meet our needs very well. Thank you for putting in so much effort.'*

• **Summarise all agreements in writing** and agree it with the individual. Then either send him a hard copy or an email.

• **Help him to see the big picture or overview.** Show him where his responsibilities fit in with others' responsibilities using diagrams. He finds this hard to do for himself.

• **Give instructions in step-by-step form.**

Wrong: *'Do a plan for the PDR project.'*

Right: *'Identify the equipment needed for the PDR project. Phone the manufacturers and find out the cost for each piece of equipment and its lead-time. Find out the deadline required by Arnold Simpson. Give me the information by Wednesday 19th.'*

• **Do not get upset about strange misunderstandings.** It's not you! This happens because they tend to remember a small detail of a conversation, whereas most people remember the gist. Listen to what they have to say. Apologise for the misunderstanding. Explain what you really meant. Take a deep breath and move on.

 ## What not to do

• **Give very short answers to their questions.** The shorter your answers, the longer the conversation will be. He will think you are not listening (which may be true). He will assume you do not care (which may also be true). True or not, these beliefs will make his behaviour even more extreme.

• **Give vague instructions.** Never do this, as it's likely nothing will happen.

• **Don't speak to him for long periods of time.** He will think you are ignoring them and often take offence.

- **Put him with other very-detail-orientated people** who cannot see the big picture either. Strangely, they will often have very low opinions of each other. They will find it hard to understand each other and continually criticise each other.

Theory

This is a more common set of behaviours than you might think. It seems to come from an extreme orientation to detail with no flexibility to see the big picture. All the symptoms stem from this lack of flexibility and being stuck in the detail.

Imagine a long cardboard tube, the kind you get inside a roll of wrapping paper. Suppose you could only view the world through this tube and you had to find your way from your home to the nearest shop. This is the world of a person who can only see detail. The very small view of the world makes long term planning and prioritising extremely difficult. It makes seeing the big picture almost impossible.

It also makes linking separate events together very hard. Understanding the context of situations and actions becomes mainly a matter of chance.

Misunderstandings occur easily because these people will remember a very small part of a conversation, or home-in on one sentence in an email. They will misinterpret it – often by taking it literally – and frequently take offence where none was intended.

Once they have a problem to deal with, that is all they can see and it occupies all their thoughts. They can't 'see round it' or 'get over it' because the scope of their view is so limited. They need help in order to do this.
However, once they have got past a problem, it is out of their mind and they will be already concentrating on the next small area.

These people often see themselves as very reliable because, in their small area of focus, they are doing exactly what they think they should be doing. Things outside that area are simply not in their consciousness.

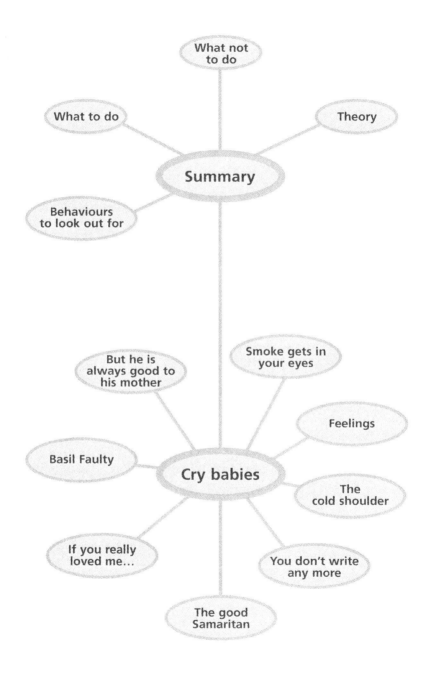

CHAPTER THREE

Cry babies

Understanding emotional people

Here is another group of people that you may have trouble dealing with. I certainly did.

I called Charlie, my PA, and asked her if she fancied a trip to Santa Barbara. I said we could do a spot of shopping and perhaps get a dip in the pool too, if we were lucky. Charlie agreed like a shot, even though she was four months pregnant. Then I told her we would be going on a course. We booked our places and the organisers were delighted that some of their delegates were coming so far – all the way from England.

The journey started with my drive down to London. I stayed there overnight and we set off early in the morning for Heathrow. The traffic was exactly as you might expect for a weekday, at the beginning of the rush hour. We found the car park we had booked into, and caught the plane without incident. Charlie and I spent the thirteen hour flight, happily watching two Harrison Ford films. We didn't bother to sleep. We were on holiday.

Then it all started to go wrong. We arrived at Los Angeles airport and waited an hour for our luggage. I have no idea whether this is usual at Los Angeles; no one else seemed surprised. Then we spent another hour negotiating escalators, walkways, car parks and finally a shuttle bus – to get to the car hire company, which felt like it was on the other side of town. We then spent another thirty minutes queueing to get our car. By now we were exhausted.

To cap it all, we then sat bumper to bumper for nearly two hours, trying to get out of LA. I don't like driving on the wrong side of the road, and have hardly ever driven automatics, so it was quite a strain. The course started at 8pm – but despite everything, we arrived with ten minutes to spare.

We were both ravenously hungry by this time – but had resisted the urge to stop for food on the way, in case we were late. Charlie was noticeably pregnant too, and while I wanted to eat, she *needed* to. We had presumed that there would be something to eat on arrival at the conference. It was scheduled for 8pm, after all.

How wrong we were.

The organisers were well aware of our journey arrangements and had said how impressed they were that we were coming so far. However, having told them we'd had a long and exhausting journey, we were offered no food at all. Eventually, we felt compelled to ask for something – anything! They managed to rustle up two small carrots, about twenty nuts and a couple of biscuits, to share between the two of us.

We went into the course room, and were told that the session would be two hours long. To say that those hundred and twenty minutes dragged would be kind. If I'd been doing the training myself, I could have packed the content into half an hour at the most.

At several points during this lengthy evening, the woman leading the course, Agnes, talked about the different personality styles we had come to learn about. She explained that her particular profile was very sensitive.

'I know how you feel,' Agnes intoned, staring meaningfully at each of us in turn for what seemed like hours. 'I am connected to you all.'

By this point I was feeling very tired and frustrated by the slow pace of the training. 'Good,' I thought to myself. 'If you know how I feel, perhaps you will do something about it.'

There was no change in pace and no acknowledgement of our feelings. This happened several times during that long evening. If anything, the pace seemed to have ground to a halt. I thought I might die before it finished. As a trainer, and someone with many years' experience in giving feedback, I mulled over the possibilities. I ran a few choice phrases through my mind. However, I realised I was very tired by now – and I recognised my tendency to sarcasm. It would be safer to say nothing at this point, but speak up the next morning (we still had two more days to go).

The next morning, over breakfast, I discovered that many others had found the pace very slow and were also surprised that the trainers had not asked Charlie or myself whether we might like to go to bed, given our long day and obvious tiredness.

I gave the trainers some feedback and was told in no uncertain terms that they knew what was best for us as far as training was concerned.

Later that morning, Agnes again told us that she knew exactly how we felt and was connected with us all. I am convinced she believed this wholeheartedly – so that left me with two alternatives: either she understood my feelings perfectly but chose to ignore them completely (along with most other people's) or she had got it wrong.

I personally believe the second option to be the truth.

Smoke gets in your eyes

My eyes had been opened to a new kind of person. I had read a book (*Human Dynamics* by Sandra Seagal and David Horne) about different personality types, and thought it had merit. The book describes a framework for understanding the way people take in and process information. Although I am not sure how valid this model is, it does give some very different and useful ways of understanding others. In order to learn more about it, you would have to read the book too – but very briefly, my understanding of it is that we can take in information in three different ways:

• We think
• We feel
• We have a physical experience

We also process information in one of these three ways. What happens is that we take information in using one route and process it using another. So there are some people who *think* and then *do something physical*. They are called *Mental Physical*. You also get people who *do something physical* (to gather the information) and then *think*. They are called *Physical Mental*. On the other hand there are people who *feel something* and then *do something*. They are called *Emotional Physical*.

It's the *Emotional Physical* people I was interested in. After reading about these people, I tried out some different approaches with them.

Instead of working through things logically as I had in the past, I focused on their *feelings*. These are people who, they say, take in all their information as emotions. Then they *do* something in response to the information such as feeling frustrated or upset. They simply take in information (as emotions) and then react. Notice there is no *thinking* stage in that process.

My personal view is that these people have much stronger emotions than others. This means that the emotions overwhelm them and send a stronger signal than other information they may be receiving. I think they find it impossible to ignore these emotions and feel compelled to act upon them. Sometimes when the emotions are very strong, they just freeze. Now, this can happen to any of us, as you will know. Here is where I depart a little from this theory.

I find Daniel Seigel's work more compelling. He talks about going outside your window of tolerance for a particular emotion. When this happens, you lose control. And this can happen to anyone. I think, though, there is a group of people who are far more prone to being outside their window of tolerance than others. You will find more about Daniel Siegel's work in the chapter on Rhinos (or insensitive people).

Going back to the very emotional behaviour, I had come across a number of people who seemed to fit this profile before my trip to Santa Barbara. However, I had never seen a large group of these people at one time. Until I went to Santa Barbara.

At the end of the course, each group in turn was asked to go up to the front of the room so that the rest of us could ask them questions. This was fascinating. Agnes, the course leader, explained how you could tell the profile of a person from her eyes. I was doubtful. But when Agnes moved on to stand twenty-five people together side by side, it was clear that she had been right. Every person in the line shared that very watery-eyed look that makes you think she is about is about to burst into tears. An expression that wouldn't look out of place on a rabbit.

Hearing how these watery-eyed people viewed the world was a revelation to me. They were all convinced that they understood and felt everyone else's feelings totally. They empathised with everyone and would not accept that they might occasionally be wrong. Being connected to people was of paramount importance and they were insulted if they thought you did not want, also, to be connected to them. Pennies began to drop. Now I understood how I had unwittingly offended (probably hundreds of) people.

One woman in the line, Hillary, gave a startling example. She explained in a martyred tone how she had helped a colleague to do something. Her whole body was tense, like a bow about to fire an arrow. Then she paused meaningfully as if she were to pull the arrow from her quiver.

'You won't believe what she did.' Hillary's voice pierced the air with its sense of injustice.

I held my breath, as did everyone else in the room. We waited for the awful conclusion.

'She thanked me,' Hillary paused while she drew breath (I thought this was just for effect, but have since revised my opinion) '...by email!'

There were gasps of horror from her emotional peers. There were looks of confusion from the rest of us. I thought I had misunderstood. Charlie glanced in my direction and raised her much-exercised eyebrows. Finally I could stand it no longer. I asked her what the problem was with the email, expecting her to say it was rude or curt. It was neither of these things; the problem was that it was an email, not a personal face-to-face meeting. I was astonished and found myself mentally totting up scores of people I could have unwittingly offended.

Others described how they had been offended by seemingly harmless acts from countless thoughtless ordinary individuals. I sat next to a monk during this part of the day. He turned to me and whispered: 'This group is very high maintenance.'

Feelings
Feelings and emotions make up the whole world for these people, according to the theory – and I believe them. Now.

I once worked with a woman, Sandy, who fell into this category. She would get terribly upset over some minor problem, or over something I just couldn't understand. This happened on an almost weekly basis. Each time it happened I would try to sort out the problem in a cold logical way. I would analyse the facts, look at what had happened and work out what the objective was. I would identify where the problem or misunderstanding had occurred and design a new system to make sure it didn't happen again. This whole process, to which I was totally dedicated, would sometimes continue over days.

I agonised over each email or conversation. I would turn the events over and over in my mind. Then, out there in the land of Santa Barbara sunshine, I came across a different way of understanding the world and it was a complete revelation to me.

One day Sandy and I had a meeting to discuss progress on various projects. One of these projects involved her getting a brand new, top-of-the-range computer. Her old one was being passed on to a new employee called Jaswinder. I was not entirely happy with this arrangement as I thought Jaswinder deserved the new equipment rather than Sandy. However, Jaswinder was perfectly happy to take over the old machine, so against my better judgement I had agreed. Like me, I am sure Sandy's response to my questions about the progress in this area, would surprise you.

Every time I asked Sandy about when she expected to pass her old computer to Jaswinder, I received all kinds of excuses and lots of aggressive behaviour. It seemed that Sandy thought I was deliberately poking my nose in where it wasn't welcome, and that I had no right to ask. I was met with evasion and anger and was at a loss to understand what was going on. I had assumed that Sandy would be delighted to be (quite undeservedly) getting a brand new machine.

Then I remembered what I had recently learned about emotional people. Instead of launching into my usual logical argument, I asked Sandy how she felt. She stopped in her tracks. She could not find the words for it, but at least I was out of her line of fire for a short while. I tossed in a few suggestions: *upset, angry, frustrated, worried?* As I used the word *worried* I saw a look of recognition on her face. Great, I was getting somewhere.

The next step was to help her link her feelings with the events in the real world. I searched around for what she could be worried about. After several tries, I remembered that there was a bug in one of the software packages that she was working on. I asked Sandy if the bug was sorted out yet. It wasn't. I asked her if she was embarrassed to be handing over the old computer with a bug on it that she hadn't managed to get fixed yet.

I could hardly believe the change in her. Sandy's shoulders dropped back down to their usual level, she stood up straight and smiled.

'Yes,' she said in a light airy way. It was the sort of reply you would give to a shop assistant who asks you if you'd like another carrier bag. I was amazed.

'We're paying Jaswinder lots of money because she will be sorting out exactly those problems,' I pointed out.

'I'll get it parcelled up tomorrow,' said Sandy with a cheerful smile. That was the end of the matter. It had taken less than five minutes, an eighty per cent improvement on my best previous time.

The cold shoulder

Leanne, a very skilled computer consultant, asked me to help her with one of her colleagues, Robyn. Leanne had once been a professional bodyguard and had a strong, lean, mean look about her, like someone off a gangster film. However, I found Leanne to be an efficient and reasonable person and I liked dealing with her. Leanne had been completely startled by Robyn's behaviour in a meeting they had had recently.

Robyn had asked Leanne to meet her for coffee in a hotel, for a meeting. She had not said what it was about. When Leanne arrived at the hotel and walked up to Robyn, it was as if a bomb had gone off. Robyn accused Leanne of ignoring her and giving her the cold shoulder. Leanne had no idea what Robyn was talking about. They had worked together a few times in the past and Leanne had always understood that they got on quite well.

You don't write any more

Leanne asked for some examples of what Robyn meant. Robyn pointed out that Leanne did not send her emails on a weekly basis. This confused Leanne; why should Leanne send a weekly email when she had nothing to say to her?

Robyn said that she herself sent Leanne an email at least once a week. Leanne confessed to me that she deleted most of them without reading them. Robyn also complained that Leanne never sent her cards. Leanne explained to me that Robyn often sent her cards. Mostly they were large colourful items, sometimes with printed messages, sometimes with personal greetings. Sometimes they were just to say thanks for meeting up, other times they seemed to be for nothing at all as far as Leanne was concerned.

By far the worst example Robyn cited was Leanne's response to the question *how are you?* Robyn proudly explained that she herself always gave a full answer to this question. She gave details of what she had been doing, how she was feeling, how her family were and described significant recent incidents. She complained that all Leanne ever said was *fine.*

Robyn found this response deeply offensive and rude. To her it showed a complete lack of care and compassion. It showed (quite correctly as Leanne admitted) that Leanne was not prepared to share details about her life with Robyn. To Robyn this was a betrayal because she had shared information about her life and expected Leanne to reciprocate.

Robyn gave a specific example. Robyn had become so upset by this *deliberate rebuff* as she saw it, that she had decided that the next time Leanne asked her how she was she would respond with *fine* just to teach Leanne a lesson – so she would learn just how offensive it was.

Leanne told me that she remembered the conversation vividly. Unfortunately her interpretation of the encounter was completely different. Leanne thought that she had made tremendous progress with Robyn because for the first time Robyn had given her back the short answer she had been hoping for all along! Robyn's side of events stunned her.

She had no wish to offend Robyn, but found herself very annoyed by what she saw as time-wasting idle chit-chat. She also had no desire to share details of her personal life with someone she felt was not a close friend. She did not see that she was obliged to share these details as a kind of trade just because Robyn had told her about *her* life. Leanne would prefer that Robyn did not share such intimacies in the first place. Leanne was almost embarrassed by all the detail she would receive.

Leanne saw the sharing more as a burden and a tedious, time-wasting task.

It was clear that Robyn was a person to whom being liked was very important. She judged this connectedness in various ways. She expected people to tell her about their lives and problems. She expected that they would email her with their news on a regular basis. And she judged them according to the way they responded when she asked them *how are you?*

When Robyn did not get the response she wanted, she simply turned up the volume on her connection-making process.

Leanne, on the other hand, was a person who liked to get a task done. She was friendly when she thought it was appropriate, but did not contact people to tell them about personal matters. She shared those details only with a very small group of close friends and did not take up time at work doing it.

She saw this kind of interaction as a waste of time and an annoyance. To her, a successful interaction was short and focused with clearly stated objectives and agreed actions. This may make her sound cold. I didn't find her cold; I found her excellent to work with (which should give you some clues about my own preferences here).

So how did Robyn and Leanne resolve their differences? I talked to them individually first and helped them to understand the different behaviours they were displaying and the different way each of them saw the world.

Once they had understood how difficult their behaviour was for each other, they were both keen to work at it. When we met as a group, we discussed some of the previous events and how they had each interpreted them. We talked about what each of them thought they were trying to achieve by, for example, in Robyn's case, giving more and more details about her home life, and in Leanne's case giving very short, business-like answers.

We also talked about how they felt about it. Robyn found it hard to believe Leanne's feelings at first, because they were so different from hers. Leanne had been completely stunned by Robyn's interpretation of the world.

To their credit, once they saw what was going on and how they had both made each other's behaviour worse, they both began to laugh. With each new example, the laughter increased. Ultimately, they agreed to do their best to understand each other more and to adapt their behaviour to suit the other person. They also agreed not to be offended or annoyed by each other's behaviour.

They agreed to give each other feedback when it was necessary and to listen to the feedback they were given.

I was very happy with this solution and know they have since worked together successfully on a few projects. They still sometimes find each other's behaviour annoying or upsetting, but are now able to discuss it sensibly and move on.

The Good Samaritan

When I was a manufacturing director, there was a woman in the production department, Joan, who was having many problems at home. She was clearly very upset about it and getting depressed. Some of her colleagues had approached me and told me of their concerns. One of them felt she might try suicide.

Joan certainly looked depressed, She had large black rings under her eyes and her whole face seemed to sag. Her thin shoulders were rounded and drooping and even her clothes looked dull and unhappy. She had the walk of a condemned prisoner.

I talked with Joan. It was a struggle for me: I had no idea how to help her myself, so I suggested she talk to the Samaritans. She was reluctant to do this but agreed to try if I called them and found out how to go about it. She wanted to know if she could see them face to face.

So I called the number from the phone book. Here's how the conversation went:

Me: *'There's a woman in my department who seems very depressed and we are all very concerned about her. She would like to know if she could see someone from the Samaritans in person.'*

Samaritan: *'How do you feel about this?'*

Me (confused): *'Well, I'm concerned. Can she come to see you?'*

Samaritan (in very concerned tone): *'When you say concerned, what do you feel?'*

Me (more confused): *'Well, just concerned. So, does she have to make an appointment?'*

Samaritan (in smooth concerned tone): *'When these kinds of things happen, it affects you in different ways; how is it affecting you?'*

Me (getting frustrated): *'Well, I'm worried, but I just need to know how she makes an appointment to see you.'*

Samaritan: *'So you are worried. How does that feel?'*

I put the phone down at this point.

Just so you don't worry, Joan survived – she did speak with the Samaritans and they were a great help, I understand.

So what's happening here? This is the same situation that we saw with Robyn and Leanne. I am trying to take action and sort out the problem; the Samaritan is trying to empathise, because that's what she does best. She is making a connection – one that I don't want. I thought that perhaps she thought I was really talking about myself and using Joan as an excuse. But this may not be the case. For a person with this profile, these events are very upsetting – so she may genuinely believe that it's not me, and still feel she needs to ask me about my own feelings.

To me this behaviour is extremely frustrating. I just want an *action*. I have since discovered that my behaviour made her behaviour worse. The more I tried to get an action, the more she talked about feelings. Had I talked a bit about feelings it would have been much easier.

If you really loved me...

I worked for many years with the head of a big department at a research institute. Joel was a man with a multicultural background. His grandparents all came from different countries. He was tremendous fun to work with, lively and intelligent. The rest of his department were rather subdued in comparison. They were only ever seen in dark grey suits. He never wore grey. His wife remains one of the most elegant people I have ever met, even into her retirement, a distinguished researcher in her own right.

One day, Joel called me and asked if I could help him with a tricky decision. I asked what it was.

'I've decided to give Toby the deputy job and I need to know how to tell Alan,' he said.

I could hardly believe my ears. Toby was a very unsuitable candidate for the post he described.

'What are your criteria for promoting Toby?' I asked and braced myself.

'Well, he expects to get it and he'd be so disappointed if he didn't – I couldn't bear to tell him,' Joel confessed.

'So your criterion is emotional blackmail,' I weighed in with my left hook.

'I suppose so. Can you come in this afternoon to help me with it?'

I dashed over and we hammered out a set of sensible criteria based on the skills required for the job. Needless to say, Toby did not meet the criteria. In fact, the only department head who came close was someone Joel hadn't even considered.

It would be easy to criticise Joel for his original decision, and I was unable to resist. But we all do this. The thought of having to tell someone something we know will upset him or her can be too much for many of us, so we often give in. I think if we knew how to deal with this situation more effectively we wouldn't have to find ourselves giving in.

As soon as you have given in once, you have set your foot on a very steep downhill slope. With each step it becomes harder to climb back up again. When at last you discover yourself at the bottom, it's too late. What you then do is explode because you have reached the end of your tether. This causes much more upset than necessary. Or, worse, you continually live with the annoyance that the other person has forced you into your decision against your will.

In fact you have allowed it to happen – almost encouraged it.

Here's what to do using Joel's example. Imagine you are Joel:

Explain the facts:

'Toby, as you know the deputy director post is vacant and I have been looking at the candidates for filling it.'

Explain your criteria for making the decision:

'I have identified a set of skills required. Let's go through them individually.'

Ask how they feel about the criteria (I do mean feel):

'How do you feel about these?'

Go through it in more detail:

'Which of these skills do you have? At what kind of level?'

By this time the other person will start to work out the solution for himself, but in a way that is much gentler than you just telling him straight out:

'Toby, you haven't got the job.'

Basil Fawlty

There was a band in Nottingham called Medium Medium who used to play on a Sunday night. Of all their songs, my favourite included the lines:

It's not what you say; it's the way that you say it
It's not what you pay; it's the way that you pay it

You may remember John Cleese as Basil Fawlty giving Manuel, the unfortunate waiter from Barcelona, some very direct feedback. He taps Manuel on the forehead with a spoon and says: 'You're a waste of space.'

We all laugh at this because we know we would like to give feedback like that, but we wouldn't really do it in practice. Would we? Think again.

I came across a case where a man, known as JC, had given some feedback to Marianne when she left his department. As a result Marianne went home that evening and did not return to work for six months. She had been completely devastated by the feedback.

'Your time management skills are appalling, you have no management skills to speak of and your staff are poorly organised. You do not know how to negotiate and you do not complete projects on time,' repeated Marianne to me one day after she had returned to work.

'That's what JC said to me,' she said, and she got out her handkerchief.

JC had been adamant that the feedback was accurate and needed to be given. It was true that there were concerns in all those areas. However, there are other ways to give people feedback. The method JC used is completely counter-productive, especially for a person with the emotional profile of Marianne.

An easier and more effective method is to take specific situations as they arise and talk about what needs (or needed) to be achieved each time.

For example:

'Marianne, do you remember project 375? We needed all the results by the end of February and it was completed at the end of March. Looking back, what do you think you could do differently in the same situation next time, to make sure that happens?'

Or, better still:

'Marianne, you remember project 375? As you know, we missed the deadline. What can you do on project 427 to make sure we hit it this time?'

Followed by:

'What skills do you think you need to improve or learn? How can I help?'

But he is always good to his mother

Something that used to annoy me a great deal until I understood it better, was a habit of one of my colleagues, Danny. He would criticise another colleague, say how useless he was, how annoying, and how he had messed up something – and then, at the end, say *but I really like him* or *he's a good bloke*.

This always struck me as being rather like when people refer to a gangster or violent criminal and then finish up by adding hopefully: *but he is always good to his mother.*

How is this relevant? Why do they say it? The reason is that liking someone and them liking you is more important than what they do, in the mind of an emotional person.

I remember one particular emotional person berating a colleague whom she worked with closely. In Jane's estimation he was cold and unfeeling. I asked her what he did in his spare time.

'Oh, a lot of charity work with disabled children,' Jane replied as though it was of no significance at all.

'If he'd just smile occasionally…' she went on to say. 'I'm sure he's a nice person really,' she added in a wholly unconvincing tone.

I believe the kind of behaviour displayed by Jane stems from her need to be liked by everyone. These people assume that the rest of the population feel the same. Of course most people think that everyone thinks as they do. Perhaps I should say that it never occurs to most people that other people are not like them.

So a person who really needs to be liked will say things that they think will make others like them – like saying how nice others are (even when they are not). This can come across as rather strange to people who don't see the world in this way. It may annoy you or seems strange – but just ignore it.

I remember my old boss saying to me once that *everyone wants to be popular*. He said this as though it were a proven fact. He was explaining to me how to be a good manager. I remember being quite surprised by the statement. It was quite clear to me that, sometimes, as a manager, you have to do things that are unpopular. That doesn't mean you should go out of your way to do unpopular things.

Summary

Behaviours to look out for

Watery eyes
Once you start to notice this it will be a very obvious sign. It's a look that seems to indicate the person is about to burst into tears. They may be about to, or they may not.

Hardly any task-focussed behaviour
They will be most concerned about feelings – their own and other people's.

The conviction that they know what you are feeling
They will be sure about this and may even tell you how you are feeling, or were feeling at a certain time.

They may misinterpret your feelings
When this happens it can be very frustrating. They can be completely convinced you feel something that you don't. Often, if you contradict them, they won't believe you.

Their over-riding concern is to be connected with people
This seems to be a need just as strong as the need for food and water.

Easily upset
Things that others are unaware of can upset these people.

Being liked and liking people is more important than the task
You will often hear these people criticise another quite severely and then add But I do really like him or But he's a lovely person as if this makes it all right. In their mind, it does. Being a nice person is more important than getting the task done.

What to do

- **Ask her how she feels.** Whatever happens you must do this first. Failure to do so can result in hours of fruitless conversation and all kinds of recrimination.

- **If you are able to talk about your own feelings,** so much the better.

- **Help her to work out what her feelings are.** Sometimes people find it very hard to work out what they are feeling while this strong emotion is overwhelming them. I suspect it's a bit like being blinded by a very strong light.

a. You can help her by making a few guesses: Do you feel *sad, upset, frustrated, miserable, terrified…?* When you get the right one, she will usually know. (The problem for people who don't have this profile is that they don't have a very large vocabulary for feelings. To help you out if you are one of these people, there is a list of feelings in the appendix).

b. Help her to relate her feelings to what has happened. Sometimes people find this really hard. It's just the same as someone with a crossword clue that they can't work out. Once someone tells them the answer, it's obvious. Should this happen, you might try a few suggestions: *Is it because you can't fix this bug? Are you upset because you wanted to go on the trip and now Boris is going instead? Are you frustrated because you need this tape and it isn't ready yet?*

c. You will be amazed how, once you have helped her to find the correct interpretation, her mood will change.

• **Next help her to identify what she needs.** Negative feelings are a signal that you have an unmet need. It could be anything. Many people never work that out, and go around with bags full of unmet needs for most of their lives.

Needs are different to wants. The *need* is to do with what you have to *achieve*. The want is how you *achieve* it. For example:

Want: *I want some chocolate*
Possible need: Hunger, comfort, attention, energy or many other things.
No one really *needs* chocolate (no, really, they don't!).

Want: *I want his job*
Possible need: Status, attention, money, excitement, fulfilment and many other options.

i. Ask the person:
What do you need?

ii. If you get a want instead ask:
How will that help you?

iii. Keep asking that question till you get to the need.

- **Help her to identify an action.** Sometimes just listening and helping her to work all this out is more than enough. Other times, it will be useful to help her to identify an action to fulfil the need.

- **If that doesn't work, ask her how she wants to feel.** This can be easier for these people than working out what the need is. Then help her to identify what needs to happen so that she gets the feeling she wants.

What not to do

- **Allow yourself to be emotionally blackmailed by this behaviour.** Because these people can respond with such strong emotions, others often give in to their demands because they think the person would be very upset if they didn't. That may be true but it's not always the best basis for a decision.

- **Use factual task-orientated language.** Talk about feelings as much as you can.

Theory

The theory behind this is that these people get their information about the world through their emotions. To them this information is just as valid as scientific research or seeing something in black and white is for others.

When you see that a table is red, you know it's red. When emotional people feel that you are angry, they *know* you are angry, just as surely as you *know* the table is red. Telling them you don't feel angry seems to do no good at all.

The difficulty for some of these people is relating the feeling to what has happened in the world and then identifying what to do about it.

Sometimes their feelings will not be feelings at all – they will be ways of blaming others for the situation they are in:
I feel patronised
I feel bullied
I feel squashed
These are all ways of saying *someone else has done something to me*. Marshall Rosenberg, in his excellent book *Nonviolent Communication*, categorises feelings into three areas:
• feelings when your needs are met
• feelings when your needs are not met
• feelings that aren't really feelings, they are ways of judging or blaming others (like the examples above)

Once a person has the information in the form of a feeling, they then do something. Unless they have processed the information effectively this can cause problems. The kinds of problems I have seen are where the information has been incorrectly interpreted; thanking someone by email is interpreted as a deliberate insult; not wanting to be connected to them is an insult.

For some of these people the world must seem full of deliberately hurtful actions by others. I imagine that must be very unpleasant.

There is a list of possible emotions the Appendix.

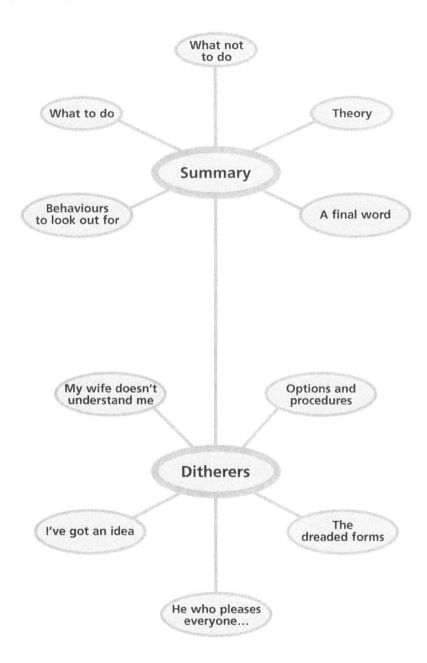

CHAPTER FOUR

Ditherers

Understanding indecisive people

I hate ditherers. I am frustrated by people who can't make up their minds. Do you know many people like this? I bet you can think of someone. Or perhaps you're not sure... these are the people who, when you are out for lunch with them, can't decide what to have from the menu. They are the people who make decisions (eventually) and then change their minds and then change them again.

A new client, Mick, asked me to design a two-day workshop for him and his department. We talked about the options and I went off to work out a plan. When we met up I presented him with the outline I had in mind. It included all the exercises and presentations he had said he needed. During the meeting he told me he had had some more ideas. I noted them down and went off to incorporate them into the plan.

When we next met he had some more ideas. These were completely contradictory to what he had first said he wanted to achieve. I told him that I could incorporate the new ideas if he wanted me to, but that it would cost extra. He said that would be fine so off I went.

At the fourth meeting, guess what? Yes, more ideas. I asked him if he remembered his original reasons for the workshop and what was important to him about the way it was done. Mick smiled at me wanly. He looked a little guilty, though slightly confused. So I referred back to my notes. In them I had recorded his requirements. I read back to him exactly what he had stipulated in our very first meeting:

'It's important that everyone gets a chance to find out about each other in a fun way, and also to find out about what the others are working on.'

'Let's go back to the original plan then,' said Mick.

When it came to the workshop, I had a woman from their HR department assisting me.

'Lilly, you will probably find that Mick will come to you with some new idea, or to change something about the workshop before we break for coffee,' I said.

'Will he?' responded Lilly, surprised.

'I guarantee it,' I said. 'When he does, just remind him of this ... I handed her a piece of paper on which I had printed Mick's original thoughts about the workshop for her.

The workshop went to plan and everyone enjoyed the activities they were working on. As we broke for coffee, Lilly came up to me with a look of amazement on her face.

'I can't believe it – Mick just asked me to add in a new activity before lunch.'

'What did you do?' I asked.

'I reminded him of the notes on the paper you gave me, and then he said it was OK, we would keep it as it was.'

'Well done,' I said with a smile.

'How did that work, then?' Lilly was intrigued.

This is a problem that we often see in people who are good at having ideas, but who are not as good at getting things done.

The difficulty for them is that they don't have a process for making decisions. For these kind of people making decisions is a process and needs a procedure and they don't like procedures.

You may be like Mick and find it hard to make decisions, or you may work with someone who shares this difficulty. Here is a procedure for making decisions:

1 Identify what you want to achieve.

2 Ask yourself what's important about how you achieve it (your criteria).

3 Identify your options for achieving it.

4 Sort the options using the criteria, coming up with the one that best meets your criteria.

5 If more than one option meets all the criteria, add more criteria or toss a coin.

Here's an example of how this works:

Let's imagine you are going through your burgeoning in-tray. You want to empty it.

The first step is being clear that by the end of the day, the in-tray will be empty. This is what you want to achieve.

Now ask yourself what's important about how you achieve it. Here are some possible criteria:

• Everything is filed somewhere sensible so you can find it again.
• It takes the minimum amount of time to do
• All your tasks are clearly identified
• All rubbish is thrown away

The next step is to identify the options. Here are a few:

• Get someone else to do it
• Throw everything into a black bin-liner
• Do it in your lunch break
• Divert your phone and get on with it
• Take it home
• Do it in three stages with breaks in between

Next you need to identify which of these options best meets your criteria. Where you have a good PA, assistant or secretary, you may find the first option would be the best. If not, depending on the height and age of the pile of papers in the tray, you may want to consider putting it all in a bin-liner.

But if you really can't decide, toss a coin. And if you don't like the choice the coin gives you, that shows that you have decided but just weren't aware of it.

You may have been a bit surprised at the last *toss a coin* step. It's quite a useful one. If all of your criteria have been met, then what you decide doesn't matter, does it? Let's imagine you are trying to decide which photocopier to buy.

Your criteria are:

- Under £1000
- Small enough to fit on top of the cupboard where it needs to go
- Colour copying
- 50 sheets per minute
- Has a 3 year warranty
- Is easy to operate

You have found three models, all at £799, all able to fit on the cupboard top, all of suitable speed, all with three year warranties and all easy to operate. The decision doesn't matter. Why waste your time on this when any of them would do the job? Toss a coin, order the machine and get on with more important things.

Many people have trouble recognising their criteria. There is a wonderful restaurant in Boston, Massachusetts, called Olives. Whenever I go to the *Learning and the Brain* Conference, which is held there twice a year, I make sure I have at least one meal in that monument to good eating.

It is always difficult for me to decide what to have. Should I go for something I have not had before? Or should I have the fantastic Falling Down Chocolate Cake pudding again – which I know to be heaven on a plate?

My friend Lew and I spend hours debating our choices on the way to the restaurant. Sometimes we even discuss them by email before we get to Boston! I have that problem when I'm in a good restaurant: I want to try all the wonderful dishes.

It's the same in the restaurant as anywhere else – you need clear criteria. In a restaurant these could be:

- The cheapest
- A vegetarian option
- Low fat
- Something I haven't tried before
- A favourite vegetable or meat
- Something I know I like
- The most unusual (this is my most frequent criterion for a restaurant)

Once you have decided on one or more criteria, then life gets easier.

Options and procedures

I used to work with a consultant called Christine. She was probably the most indecisive person I have ever known. On top of that, she seemed to do everything at the last minute – which usually meant extra work for me. I must also give her the credit for being very creative – if only a small percentage of her ideas had been put into practice she would be rich by now.

She found it very hard to let me have the notes she had written for a course in time, which meant that everything had to be done in a great rush at the last minute. The printing would be done the night before the course and I would have to do all the formatting late in the night on the desktop publishing program because no one else had any time left to do it.

Our administrator was a very different kind of person. She was the kind who just got on with tasks and couldn't understand why Christine delivered late so consistently. So Liz would phone Christine when things got urgent.

'You must email me the notes by 5pm today,' Liz would say.

Nothing happened.

Liz even tried telling Christine what the rules were weeks beforehand:

'You must email me the notes by 27th July. I have scheduled in a day to format them on 28th,' she tried.

Again, this did not work. If anything it seemed to make the problem worse. Here's why:

People who behave like this have what is called an *options* pattern of behaviour. This means they are very good at thinking of options and ideas, but many of these people are not nearly so good at getting things done. At the other end of the scale are the *procedural* people. These people get things done. They put a task on their list, and, when they get to that task, they do it.

The trouble is that when a *procedural* person like Liz tries to get an *options* person like Christine to do something, she is restricting the options available. This is infuriating for the options person. An options person's motto is *rules are there to be broken*. The more you try to get them to stick to rigid rules, the less they are likely to.

This all makes life very difficult if you are working with someone like this and you need her to follow certain procedures. So, how do you do it? You have to give her options within the procedure.

One of my clients, Andy, a manager who believed in hard work and discipline, tried insisting that his people wrote their reports at particular times.

'You must write this report on Thursday afternoon,' he would say.

This caused all kinds of ill feeling. I suggested he try an alternative:

'I need this report for Friday morning. What are the options?'

His very options-orientated people then were able to give all kinds of ideas, for example:

- Do the report at home
- Reschedule some other work so it could be done
- Miss a meeting and do it then
- Do it while a test was running
- Work late one evening to do it
- Do it over lunch

Andy discovered that the response was much better. The reports were done on time.

This was because people were given choices and were told what needed to be achieved, not how to do it. Too often, we focus on telling others what to do rather than give them some responsibility for how they tackle the problem. In some situations this works very well and gives good results. In others it causes problems.

When does it work? It works with people who are behaving in a procedural way.

I took up riding at a much later age than most. As an adult, I suspect learning to ride is rather different than when you are young; for one thing, you are more aware of all the injuries you might sustain.

I found cantering terrifying at first. My horse always seemed to be about to charge off into the distance, and carelessly throw me off into a ditch – or worse. On these occasions, my teacher, the ever patient Dawn, would shout at me, in a voice that could be heard in the next county.

'Sit back. Hold the reins together. Relax your shoulders.' Quickly followed by:

'Are you breathing?' Then she would add one final instruction:

'Smile – look as though you are enjoying yourself.'

It would have been no good at all to give me a series of choices at this time. I just wanted to know what to do.

Let's look at a very different situation.

The dreaded forms

Most serious *options* people hate filling in forms. Not only that, but they miss things out and put answers in the wrong boxes. This all happens without the slightest extra effort on their part. In fact it happens when they are really trying hard. I know. I'm one of those people.

When we moved our mortgage to a new building society I agreed to go in and talk to the advisers. I knew we would have to fill in some horrendous form. I had an appointment with Barbara, the mortgage manager. She was a sturdy looking woman with short permed hair and gold-rimmed glasses.

I was not looking forward to the experience. We had researched the options carefully and knew this was a good deal, but it was the form-filling that I dreaded.

Barbara came to the place where I was seated and introduced herself. We shook hands and went into her office.

'You need to fill in this form before we can finalise the mortgage,' she said and put a thick manual on the desk. My heart sank.

Then to my great delight she continued:

'There are three options; you can take it home and fill it out there, you can fill it out here on the screen or we can just identify the information I don't have and I'll do it for you.'

This may sound trivial to you, but to me it was a great burden lifted from my shoulders. Naturally I chose the last option. It was all over in less than ten minutes. Not only that, but I have been promoting that building society, The Derbyshire, ever since.

There are always ways of adding in extra options to make it easier for the options person. When you feel tempted to tell them what to do, and tell them straight, you need to recognise that you are making it worse.

He who pleases everyone…

I have had many clients over the years who have complained that their managers just won't make decisions, or constantly change their minds. This behaviour causes many problems, especially when a manager is in a very senior role.

I don't think people who have not suffered from this realise quite how costly and annoying it can be. Let's look at one example:

The manager concerned had a department of several hundred people. His name was Derek. He had a long drooping beard and always wore sandals, even in the middle of winter. He would wear them with grey socks, all year round. Like many people in this kind of role, he was recruited for his technical expertise, not his skill in managing others. In fact Derek had previously only ever managed a secretary. The HR manager involved in the recruitment, Susie, counselled against his appointment but was told he would be a real asset to the company because of his many contacts in the field and his excellent reputation due to his research record.

I had known the senior management team that worked for Derek for some time. When their previous manager moved on to a wonderful new post at another company they were very sad to see him go. When they started working for Derek, they got the shock of their lives. Instead of the visionary leader to whom they had become accustomed they found themselves, instead, dealing with a man who never seemed to be able to make up his mind about anything.

Derek was a small man with a ready smile. He smiled at everyone. This made his beard shake and he looked like an old and rather expensively bred dog. Derek's smile said *I am eager to please you*. You instinctively knew that, if he had had a tail, it would be wagging. He was dying to please everyone. You are probably familiar with the old saying 'he who pleases everyone pleases no one'. This was Derek's mantra. People found his behaviour infuriating. He had one or two other problems too – one of them was that he made many mistakes but would not admit to any of them. This made him vastly unpopular with his team, and also something of an object of ridicule.

Derek's manager, Morgan, was terrified of tackling the problem. When at last the HR manager persuaded him to do something, he was still very concerned. He was from the 'let sleeping dogs lie' school of management.

We had a meeting. Morgan was a thin, pale-looking individual who looked as though he didn't get enough sun. He was dressed in clothes about two sizes too big for him. I wondered whether he had shrunk at some stage in his life.

Morgan's approach was that he wanted me to coach Derek and sort him out. He did not want to get involved at all. Susie and I exchanged glances. I explained to Morgan that the problem was rather more serious than that and would need more work than just coaching. He, as the manger, would also need to put in some effort.

We knew that several people were planning to leave because they hated working for Derek and that the output of that area was around twenty per cent of any other comparable area in the company worldwide.

In the end I talked to each of Derek's direct reportees to find out what the main problems were and then I learned their views on what needed to happen. We then held some workshops where we looked at behaviours in the team and agreed what was acceptable.

Most of the time was spent focusing on how to make decisions and stick to them. This involved having a clear set of criteria. One of Derek's most unfortunate habits was to agree something in a meeting and then agree something completely different with someone else afterwards. He usually didn't even mention he had changed his mind to his team so they carried on obliviously. As I am sure you can imagine, this had caused some very difficult problems.

One of the key problems with Derek's behaviour was that he was extremely status conscious. I have noticed over the years that this focus on status can be an indicator of some very immature behaviour. Why is this?

When you were four or five, everyone bigger than you had more power than you. This is how it had been for all your life until that moment. However, as you got older, this became less and less true. Most mature people are nothing like as status-orientated as small children. I believe this to be a sign of their maturity.

When a person is as status conscious as Derek this behaviour often goes hand in hand with other immature behaviours, like very poor negotiation skills and needing to please everyone.

I think one of the reasons Derek changed his mind so often is because he was always so keen to please others. This meant that he would agree with whichever person was in front of him at the time. When faced with more than one person, he would agree with the most senior.

I decided to use Derek's high status awareness to help us. I enlisted the support of his manager and got Morgan to agree to endorse the work we had done in the workshops to Derek. To my relief it worked. Morgan told Derek he was very pleased that Derek's team had done all this useful work on decision-making and how he valued people who made decisions and stuck to them – even when it was difficult. There was quite an improvement in Derek's behaviour as a result of this. Although Morgan had to repeat his feedback on many occasions, the effort proved worthwhile.

It's unlikely that Derek will ever be a very decisive person, but, with the support of his manager, his behaviour was changed quite substantially. Changing the way you manage someone can often make a huge difference.

I've got a great idea

Another behaviour you tend to find with indecisive people is that they come up with so many ideas that they forget what they were trying to achieve in the first place. I was working with a group of creative people, and six of them were asked to spend a few hours producing a presentation that they would give to the directors. After an hour or so I went into their room to see how they were getting on.

The leader, Trevor, was at the whiteboard, pen in hand. His sandy hair was flung back and his stripy sleeves pushed up over his elbows. His arms flailed like airplane propellers. The other five team members stood at various flip charts. All were talking excitedly about what they could do and what they could put on the slides.

I asked them to tell me what they'd achieved so far. They gave me a mishmash of all kinds of things they could do and the ideas they had had.

'What is it that you need to achieve by giving this presentation?' I asked Trevor.

There was a long silence. Trevor looked down at his shoes.

'We could put this example in here...' he suggested enthusiastically.

'What do you need to achieve?' I asked again.

There were mutters of: 'Tell them about this package...' from the rest of the team.

'I think you need to persuade them to agree to the implementation of this package,' I suggested.

'Oh yes,' admitted Trevor.

I led them through a process for achieving their goal. They were able to use many of the ideas they had come up with. We agreed that only items that would help with their objective could go into the presentation.

So what we had done was very similar to the process at the beginning of the chapter – we had just done it in a slightly different order.

1 Identify what you want to achieve

2 Ask yourself what's important about how you achieve it (your criteria)

3 Identify options for achieving it

4 Sort the options using the criteria, coming up with the one that best meets your criteria.

On this occasion, Trevor and his people identified the options first (step three), then I moved them back to step one and then steps two and four. This is a longer way round, but it is still possible to retrieve a situation by drawing people back to what they need to achieve, and then agreeing a set of criteria.

My wife doesn't understand me

These problems can happen at home too. A friend of mine told me how her husband never made decisions – so she always had to nag him into it. Of course, as you will now know, this behaviour was making him worse. Vanessa, an old friend and the kind of person who got things done, would be infuriated by Dennis, her husband, who never made decisions and was very slow to get things done.

As a result, she found herself nagging him – something she hated to do, but she did not know any other way of dealing with the situation.

I hate the use of the word nagging. It has all kinds of implications and seems to give the impression it's the fault of the woman. I don't think it's anyone's fault. It's just a way of doing things that grows from two very different behaviours.

When you need an indecisive person to do something, you need to give him choices and options. Otherwise he will feel restricted and become very hard to pin down. You also have to let him live with the consequences of his behaviour instead of catching all his mistakes and thereby enabling him to continue being 'useless'.

I know this can be very hard sometimes. I once told the delegates on a course that, when I went away, my husband would often ask me for a list of jobs that needed to be done. I would give him a list and when I got back, they would all be done. I was faced with a group of open-mouthed women. Not a single one of them had experienced this happy situation.

So, if you have a partner who is indecisive, here's what you do:

1 Explain what you need

2 Ask them what the options are

3 Agree what's important about it (the criteria for making the decision)

4 Let them make the choice

5 Leave them to it

6 Accept the consequences – that is, if they do not do it

For example:

You: *'The washing machine has broken down. Your shirts need washing ready for Friday. What are the options?'*

Partner: *'Well, I could fix it or we could get someone in or you could go to a laundrette.'*

You: *'Or you could go in a shirt that isn't clean. (Keep the sarcasm out of your voice, this IS an option!) What's important here?'*

Partner: *'That I have a clean shirt for Friday.'*

You: *'And that it's done in the minimum time as I am working late for the next two days. So what do you think?'*

Let your partner decide. If he or she agrees to do it and then fails, do not step in; let him or her deal with the consequences. It will be hell that first time – but you will reap the benefits long term.

It's also important to remember that some things just aren't as important to other people as they are to you. It may be that you just have to do them yourself sometimes.

Summary

Behaviours to look out for
Procrastination
People delaying decisions.

Frequent changing of mind
Agreements are made and then changed time and time again.

No decisions made at all

What to do
- **Find the criteria.** You need to help the other person to find out what his criteria for making the decision are. You do this by asking: 'What's important about...' whatever he says he needs. Where appropriate, you might like to add your own criteria.

- **Then make the decision.** Once you have the criteria, you use these to help the person make the decision. This is done by weighing up any options against the criteria you have identified:

You: *'What's important to you about this date?'*

Other: *'It needs to be before Christmas and a day the whole team can make.'*

You: *'What else?'*

Other: *'I guess we will need a day when the board room is available.'*

You: *'Anything else?'*

Other: *'Oh yes, not a day when we have a rush on in production, so not the month end.'*

You: *'Is that it?'*

Other: *'Yes.'*

- **Offer him a series of options** (if appropriate) for how you are going to do it. 'I could check the diary, ask Graham to do that, or we could look now on the system. What would suit you best?'

- **Go through how you have arrived at the decision.** The dates that were available for the team were 4th, 15th, 19th, 21st and 28th. The boardroom is only available for 21st and 28th. The 28th is too near the end of the month so we have booked the 21st.

- **Write the criteria down.** If the person changes his mind, remind him of what it was he wanted to achieve, and what he said was important.

What not to do

- **Try to force the person to follow a procedure.** When dealing with this person in general, do not force this person into one solution. This is unlikely to work and will generally make him worse. Even being able to offer him small amounts of choice will help – however, make sure your criteria are there:

'I need the report by Friday – would you like to fax it, email it or give me a hard copy?'

Theory
Making decisions involves a process. Very often people who find it difficult to make decisions are missing a step in that process. That step is identifying their criteria. By helping them to discover what these are, you will help them to make a decision.

Telling a person what she must do can often make things worse. If she feels forced down a particular route, she will often change her mind later. Make sure you always give an element of choice, somewhere in your dealings with her. This is because extreme behaviours lead to more extreme behaviour.

You might be at the other end of the scale here – very procedural – in which case your behaviour when dealing with an options person will make her worse. The more procedural you are, the more options-orientated she will become. And you will become more procedural. So it goes on.

A final word
In situations like this your gut instincts will be exactly the opposite of what you need to do.

CHAPTER FIVE

Rhinos

Understanding insensitive people

One day I had a phone call from my long-standing client, Caroline, an HR manager used to dealing with people problems.

'Nancy, you're our last hope,' she said.

'Well,' I replied. 'I usually like to be described as my client's first choice, but I'll go with last choice.'

Caroline laughed.

Our last hope

Caroline was a cheerful, jovial woman in her thirties. She was very attractive with a lively personality and was always fun to work with. We had been through many difficult situations together.

Caroline then went on to describe a thorny situation: She had received a call for help from Roger, one of the managers in the company. He was having a problem with Tony. Tony was behaving rudely to customers, talked too loudly (he worked in the town library) and, so Roger said, often swore at his computer. His colleagues found this unacceptable. His customers didn't like it much either. However, his technical skills were perfectly acceptable and, when he took the time to listen to his clients, he did a good job.

I asked how long the problem had been going on. Caroline reckoned it must have lasted about eighteen years. There were no records. The local authority had brought in an appraisal system only about five years previously and all Tony's appraisals had been satisfactory.

This is a common story. Many managers find these kinds of issues very hard to deal with and tend to ignore them, hoping they will go away. They rarely do. What usually happens is that the person gets shunted from one department to another until he or she runs out of managers.

We agreed that I should talk to Roger, Tony's manager, and a meeting was arranged. A week later I went to the library and made my way to Roger's office, which was up a few dingy staircases, away from the main part of the library. Roger was a kind-hearted individual, looking forward to his retirement. He reminded me of the kind of person who would make a wonderful, if slightly batty, uncle. His clothes were dishevelled and there was a stain on his tie, which did not look recent. His glasses were held together with sticking tape just in front of his right ear. Roger was reluctant to tackle a problem and hated conflict in all its forms. He had rarely given feedback of any kind to anyone.

Next I talked to Tony's colleagues. They were a mixed bunch. Some recognised that Tony did not intend to behave offensively; others just hated him. One woman, Eleanor, was positively venomous.

'He should know better. He shouldn't behave like that,' she kept telling me.

Another colleague, Pat, was more understanding. She had worked in the library for about 20 years and would have made a good Miss Marple in an Agatha Christie novel. Her small dark eyes darted about, as if scrutinising my clothes, looking for clues. She chatted cheerfully about Tony, giving me well-observed examples of his behaviour in a manner that seemed quite objective.

'He sometimes swears at his computer,' she told me, her eyebrows slightly raised. In these situations, it's always useful to check the evidence you have been given by just one person. Sometimes what one person insists is a constant problem turns out to have been an isolated incident and you need to be sure of your facts before you take any action.

'One day I saw him hit his head on the computer; he just leaned forward and bashed his forehead on the screen,' she continued. 'I was rather embarrassed; we had customers in the library at the time. They must have heard – it was very loud.' She paused. 'I didn't know what to do.'

I needed to talk with Tony and see for myself what his behaviour was like before I could work out a plan. When I met him he seemed perfectly reasonable. We had an interesting conversation, but he did more lecturing than listening. As we talked I checked his awareness of body language. He was completely unaware of anything I did at all.

He did not seem to notice when I wanted to speak and he hardly ever left a pause that I could break into (and for me that is really saying something). When I *accidentally* dropped my pen, he made no sign that he had even noticed. Had you been in her shoes at that moment, you would probably have made some small move towards the pen to pick it up, like most people.

I decided to try letting him see himself on video. We recorded some conversations and then we watched the video. He couldn't see anything wrong with his style. I had to point out body language issues to him.

What's going on
At one of Eric Jensen's Brain Expo's in San Diego, I was lucky enough to hear Daniel Siegel speak. He was one of the keynote presenters.

Daniel Siegel talked about how we learn various behaviours, crucial to our later lives, when we are very young. Although not everyone agrees with his work, I have found it extremely useful. In his book, *The Developing Mind*, Siegel talks about seven skills we all need in order to be able to operate effectively with other humans.

These are the seven skills:

- Sensitivity
- Specificity
- Intensity
- Windows of Tolerance
- Recovery Process
- Access to Consciousness
- External Expression

You need to have a level of skill in each of these seven areas in order to be able to interact effectively with other people. I find this theory a very useful way to discern what may be going on when there are problems with a person's behaviour.

Sensitivity – do you notice it?
Most people need a minimum amount of stimulation in order for something to get their attention. This is variable depending on our state of mind. You can think of this as the difference between someone who has poor eyesight and someone whose eyesight is good. The person with the poor eyesight might not notice a warning sign that

uses small writing, but might see one that uses larger writing. It's the same with the signals we need to notice in other people.

For example, if I raised my eyebrows while you were talking to me, would you notice? The chances are that you would. This shows you have the sensitivity to pick up that stimulus. Some people do not.

Specificity – what does it mean?

Once you have noticed a stimulus – someone raising his or her eyebrows, the tone of a person's voice, for example – you need to work out what this means in the context of that situation. We are all affected by our own unique circumstances, many layers of experience and the context in which the actual event takes place. Specificity refers to the way in which we categorise the stimulus. For instance, we may see it as pleasant, unpleasant, useful, a threat and so on.

Imagine we are talking together. While you are speaking, you notice me take a deep breath. That could mean a number of different things. It could mean that I want to speak. It could mean I am surprised or shocked. Or I could be concealing a yawn. You need to specify what it means in order to carry out an interaction that works effectively.

Intensity – how strong are your feelings?

This refers to the intensity of your response to a situation, which can vary according to your state of mind. Some people feel very intense emotions (not always pleasant) when they encounter new situations. This may lead them to avoid such situations. The level of intensity depends on the amount of neurotransmitters your brain releases in response to a given stimulus.

Imagine you have a really bad day at work. On the way home you have an accident in your car. Then, when you arrive home, you open your electricity bill and find it is twice what you were expecting. As a result, the intensity of your feelings may be higher than usual. On the other hand, imagine you have won a large sum of money. You have had a good day at work. Now open that bill. The intensity of your feelings will probably be quite different.

You probably know people who over-react in many situations. You may also know people who hardly seem to respond at all to extreme events. This is often because the intensity of emotion they feel is either very high (in the first case) or very low in the second case.

Windows of tolerance – are your emotions overwhelming?

Let's imagine that we could measure the strength of our emotions on a scale from one to ten. Some people can cope with a feeling at the top end of the scale – say, ten – while others can only tolerate a five feeling or lower. We all have levels we can cope with, called *windows of tolerance*. Each window of tolerance can change depending on each circumstance.

Let's say your window of tolerance for frustration went up to six on our imaginary scale, and something caused your emotional intensity to go up to eight in frustration: you would no longer be in control. You would lose your temper. When you move outside your window of tolerance for a particular emotion your thinking and behaviour become disrupted. You are no longer able to think about issues and your mind does not respond appropriately. In some situations, you may behave more like a five-year-old than an adult.

For example, when I was a student, a friend of mine, Daisy, brought her pet to my birthday party. It was a snake. She had it round her neck rather as most people would wear a scarf. The sight of this snake pushed another friend out of his *window of tolerance*: he emitted a loud cry and leapt over the TV. He later claimed the snake had *gone for him*.

The reason he jumped over the TV instead of calmly saying: *'Please excuse me, I'm not very keen on snakes,'* and leaving the room in a dignified manner, was because he was outside his window of tolerance. He had no access to his cognitive functions and higher order thinking skills. His response was completely unthinking.

When you are outside your window of tolerance you don't have access to various parts of your brain, so you can't think effectively. The parts you don't have access to are the parts that perform the more grown-up functions such as thinking skills, reasoning, problem-solving and forward planning. Other grown-up functions include understanding that other people have needs and being able to identify them (a skill that often eludes people when they are outside their *window of tolerance*).

As your brain develops, you progressively learn more complex functions. When you were born you could not tie a shoelace or speak. When you were five you probably could not understand calculus or read very well. You may not have said *please* and *thank you* as often as your parents would have liked. We have all seen children doing things that are inappropriate – and usually we don't mind too much. When we see an adult behaving rudely or throwing a tantrum, we are less forgiving. This is because we expect people to have learned how to behave by the time they become adults.

Recovery process – how soon do you stop sulking?

When you have moved outside your window of tolerance you need to move back into it again. For some people this process is easy. They lose their temper and a few moments later they are back to normal. You probably know people who take days to stop sulking after something has upset them. Being able to *talk yourself down* quickly is a skill, and a crucial one for interacting effectively with others. It's not one everyone has.

When a child is told he cannot have a toy, it's not unusual for him to cry or to sulk for a while. Part of the responsibility of a parent or carer is to help a child learn how to deal with disappointment. A person who never learns this skill as a child will carry that lack of skill with him into adult life.

In this instance, the skill is being able to put a disappointment behind you. Another example of a poor recovery process would be someone who inappropriately bears a grudge or remains in a bad temper for long periods of time.

Access to consciousness – 'What do you mean, stop shouting!'

Are you consciously aware of your emotions and why you have them? Being consciously aware allows you to understand why you are feeling what you are feeling and to take subsequent action. When someone tells you that you're shouting, and you don't think you are, this is a sign that you are not aware of how you are feeling and how your feelings are affecting your behaviour.

External expression – does your face say what you think it says?

Do you show others the appropriate emotions? Sometimes we need to show our actual emotions, sometimes not. For example: when your aged aunt gives you a jumper she has knitted you for Christmas, in colours that are in no way complimentary to your complexion and in a style that is fifty years out of date, you may think it would be appropriate to smile and thank her.

Occasionally you may have seen something very funny (I once saw a man literally slip on a banana skin) and felt the overwhelming urge to laugh, but thought better of it. Some people are not aware of the impression they are giving – they may look confused to the rest of us when they are just listening hard. This leads to misunderstandings.

Back to Tony

Tony seemed to have little sensitivity to stimuli such as body language and facial expressions. He did not seem to have a very wide range of emotions either. His expression of his own emotions was also inappropriate at times.

This lead to many of the problems his colleagues had raised, although it's not immediately obvious why.

How many times have you felt like swearing at your computer? If you're like me, it has happened on a number of occasions. However, although I have felt like it, I've never done it when others were there. There have been times when I have felt like hitting my computer – very much like Basil Fawlty in that famous episode of *Fawlty Towers*, where he hits his car with the branch of a tree. Who can honestly say they have never felt like doing that? The difference is that most of us don't do it.

We are able to control our emotions. We are also sensitive to the hints and comments of others. When we see a raised eyebrow, we know what it means. When someone drops a hint, we understand and alter our behaviour accordingly. Roger, Tony's manager, had tried to get Tony to keep the volume of his voice down. He went on to describe one particular occasion to me.

'We were having a discussion in the library and Tony was talking very loudly. I said to him: "I don't think the people in the next room need to hear what we are saying." Tony just carried on as if I hadn't said anything,' explained Roger.

'Was there any response?' I asked.

'None that I noticed,' he said sadly. Then Roger removed his glasses and polished them, before replacing the smeared lenses on his nose.

I spoke to Roger about some of the other incidents I had talked about with his colleagues.

'Have you seen Tony hitting his head on his computer?' I asked.

'Oh yes,' said Roger. 'He does it quite often.'

'And what do you do when he does it?'

'Well, people make tutting noises and raise their eyes to the heavens. Some make comments.'

'Does anything seem to make any difference?' I asked.

'No,' he sighed. 'Nothing.'

'Have you ever seen him embarrassed?' I asked.

Roger looked surprised. 'Embarrassed?' He paused and seemed to search his mind hard. 'I really don't think I ever have, in all the years I have known him. And goodness knows, there's been plenty of opportunity.' His shoulders slumped.

Here was a key to Tony's behaviour. Let's take a moment to really think about emotions, what they are, and what they are there for. Emotions are physiological responses generated in our bodies that give us some kind of feeling. The feelings are a message from our body and tell us something. Fear tells us that there might be a threat. Sadness tells us that we have lost something. What does embarrassment tell us? It tells us that we have done something socially inappropriate. This is a very important message to understand and act upon, if we want to deal with others effectively. It is a key to learning social skills.

If you have children, ask yourself how often you have had to tell them to say 'please' (if you don't, remember how often your own parents told you). I would be prepared to bet it's more than once. We don't learn social skills from one piece of feedback. What would happen if you never told your children to say 'please'? It just wouldn't happen.

This is what had happened to Tony. Because he was insensitive to the hints people gave him *and* he never felt embarrassment (the internal message telling him he had made a social *faux pas*) his chances of learning the finer social niceties were very low. What he needed was some feedback he could see or hear that made sense to him.

One of the most effective ways of dealing with this kind of problem is to give the person feedback in a way he or she can understand. This means your method must be very clear and straightforward. The feedback needs to state exactly what we want the person to do. So we show the person the rules in a way that they, personally, can understand.

I worked with Tony's manager, Roger, on this, but he found it impossible. He was too embarrassed to use the words *Tony, you are speaking too loudly. Speak quietly.*

We only feel embarrassed when giving these people this kind of feedback because we *imagine* they will feel embarrassed. Believe me, they won't. Once you, too, understand and believe that, you can give this kind of feedback yourself.

Unfortunately, in this case, Roger just could not bear to do it. Because of this, Tony's behaviour did not change very much. Eleanor completely refused to help Tony. Her attitude was very much that it was not her responsibility so she saw no reason to make any effort. I was greatly saddened by her response, but not surprised. Many people think that others are deliberately doing things to them. They live their lives blaming others for their problems and will do nothing about it. Eleanor was one of those people.

Pat was more open to suggestions, being a naturally helpful person. She did her best to give Tony feedback, and, when Roger retired, was promoted into his position. She worked hard with Tony, but it is difficult to make up for the loss of fifty years' feedback in a few months. When the budget was cut back, Tony was given a redundancy package. He was pleased with the package, but concerned that, in his fifties, he might not find another job. However, I am pleased to say, he did find another job, working in a museum – and seems happy.

I have seen Eleanor several times since Tony left. She is never smiling and now complains about other colleagues who deliberately cause her problems.

The Star Trek fan

When I consider my most successful examples of coaching insensitive people, I notice that in every case I was always able to work with everyone involved. I have worked with the insensitive one, his or her manager and the rest of the team. Once the whole team has agreed to help, we were able to make considerable progress.

Marcel is a manager I have enjoyed working with over the years. He is one of the most considerate and effective managers I have known. His manner is modest and almost humble. He is invariably kind and thoughtful and is always trying to do the best for his team. What's more, it is no coincidence that his team members all admire and respect him. When I suggested working with the whole team and not just with the individual concerned, on a problem he had described, and which I will explain later, Marcel put it to them and asked me to come along to the meeting.

Everyone freely admitted they were annoyed by Peter's behaviour, which seemed thoughtless, rude and insensitive to them. However, when I explained a little about the background and what it was like for Peter, they showed great understanding and agreed to do all they could to help.

Peter had a similar problem to Tony, from our last example. He was extremely insensitive to hints, body language and any subtleties. He also never seemed embarrassed and was awkward on social occasions, although he never seemed to mind.

I showed the team how to give feedback in a direct and clear manner and we practised it. The important part was to give positive feedback when Peter was doing what they wanted him to do, rather than just identifying what they didn't want him to do.

Here's an example:

'Peter, when you asked us all if we would like a drink, I was very pleased. It was very helpful because I am really busy today. Thank you.'

The keys are:

- Use his name
- Identify what he did
- Explain why it was good

When you need to give feedback on the behaviours you don't want, you always need to make it clear what you do want the person to do at the same time.

'Peter, when we have visitors, please introduce everyone to them before starting the meeting.'

We often feel tempted to harp on about the things we don't want:

'Peter, you didn't introduce everyone. This is very annoying.'

This approach in giving feedback is destructive and very unhelpful. It does not explain what you want the person to do.

Once everyone had learned how to give effective feedback, we got them all together with Peter for a meeting, to devise an action plan. Everyone agreed that they would give him feedback promptly and do their best to help.

You may well be thinking that this must have been an excruciating meeting. But don't forget, Peter himself would not have been embarrassed. He was not, of course, and the meeting went very well.

Over the next few weeks I monitored his progress with his manager. Peter had some individual coaching from me and the team backed up the work we were doing by giving feedback around everything he did that was good.

During one of our coaching sessions, I discovered that Peter was a *Star Trek* fan. His favourite character was Seven of Nine from the *Voyager* series. You may not be familiar with *Star Trek* so let me give you a few details here. Seven of Nine is a woman who is half machine. She is very intelligent, but has no social skills to speak of. Her behaviour is unfeeling, insensitive and cold. In short, it is very similar to Peter's.

I asked Peter if he was familiar with Captain Picard, the captain of one of the ships in another series of *Star Trek*. He was. I suggested to Peter that, in future dealings with his colleagues, indeed with any humans, he could think about Jean-Luc Picard and ask himself what Picard would do in the same situation. In this way he would model his behaviour on someone whose skills were good.

The results were excellent. The improvement was so marked that Peter got a promotion.

There are two important points here. The first is that, if we find a way to give people feedback in a form they can understand, then we will almost certainly see improvement. This is backed up by research showing that performance can be enhanced by over 30 per cent just by giving prompt, factual feedback in an informal manner. This is from research by the Corporate Leadership Council. You can find out more about them from their web site: www.corporateleadershipcouncil.com.

The second point is that you must always find a way for a person to learn what works for *him*. Peter was not very sensitive to other people's feelings and had few 'gut' instincts. He did, however, know many episodes of his favourite TV series almost by heart. This means he had all the right information, just in a different format. Once he accessed it, life changed for him.

How not to learn to ski

Years ago I went skiing with some friends. They were all accomplished skiers and I was not. In fact, I wasn't very keen about going along at all. I had been skiing many years before and spent time at a ski-school, which seemed to specialise in helping you feel completely useless. I had fallen over many times and didn't feel as though I had learned anything at all.

This time I had decided to take some of my own medicine and get a professional coach to help me improve my skills.

My coach was amazingly good. He was in his early twenties – an engineering student and a brilliant skier. His coaching skills were superb. Within ten minutes I was feeling confident and skiing (almost) happily down quite a steep slope. He focused on telling me every time I did something good and making it clear what I needed to do. All his feedback was specific and he constantly pointed out my improvements.

At the end of the second one-hour session I was skiing down a difficult 'black' slope. I was finally enjoying the experience.

As a result of this, I decided to get another coach on our next skiing holiday. I could hardly wait.

This coach had a completely different strategy. All he did was tell me what I was doing wrong. 'Don't stick your sticks out.' 'Don't lean like that.' 'Look at these tracks, here's where your left ski left the ground, that was bad.' On it went. After three hours of this gruelling tirade I knew I would never ski well. As a kindness he then took me right to the top of the mountain.

He said this would save me money, as I wouldn't have to buy a ski pass. I am sure he thought he was doing me a favour.

He left me there. It took me the whole afternoon to get down. I couldn't face the slopes the next day. I had almost decided never to ski again.

One of my clients told me a similar story. He was a champion archer. He had won many competitions and medals. His club got a coach to help him and a few others improve their skills. The first thing the coach did was criticise virtually everything about his technique, starting with the way he pulled back the string. Within a few weeks his confidence was destroyed and he has not shot a single arrow since.

The reason this is so destructive is that it doesn't help us to know what we should be *aiming for*, only what we need to *avoid*. Then it's only by chance that we might hit upon an effective technique. Even then we may not realise it, because we are not getting feedback to tell us we've got it right.

We need to give feedback that lets a person know what they are doing well, as well as what they can do to improve further.

Let's look at a few variations on this theme:

Impervious to external stimuli

Sheila came to me for some Time Management coaching. One of the tasks taking up far more time than it should have done was her dealings with one of her administration people, Marion. Marion was efficient in her job and a valuable employee, but would not stop talking when you had her on the phone. Sheila needed to talk with Marion several times a day and felt as though she was wasting hours each week, just trying to get off the phone.

It was clear that Marion had no sensitivity to Sheila's signals that she needed to get on with her work. I asked Sheila if she had ever seen Marion embarrassed, and, sure enough, she hadn't.

Sheila did not want to upset Marion. I asked Sheila if she had ever seen Marion upset as the result of feedback.

'I have never seen her even respond to feedback,' replied Sheila.

'That's because she probably doesn't even recognise it as feedback, or understand it,' I pointed out.

Sheila was not convinced. However, she reluctantly agreed to give my strategy a go.

I suggested that Sheila simply said: *'Marion, I need to go now.'* And then put the phone down.

Later that day, Sheila called me to say it had worked fantastically well. She was delighted, and says this method still works to this day. In fact she has since recognised the same behaviour in a few others and has used the same strategy. Another benefit of this is that she no longer feels frustrated by Marion's behaviour.

Sheila is now able to value Marion more for her positive attributes. Even better, Sheila has trained her other staff in the same techniques so now they are all more efficient (and happier).

How many technicians does it take to change a light bulb?

This case was fascinating to me because it showed how a very small problem can be misinterpreted and magnified and go on to cause many other problems too.

I was asked to see a technician, Frank, who, I was told, was lazy, sly and untrustworthy. His manager, Terry, had risen through the ranks and knew Frank's job inside out because he himself had done it for ten years.

He told me how Frank took three or four times longer than necessary to do everything, would never commit to anything, and was completely untrustworthy. I can't say I was looking forward to being in a room on my own with him.

At our first meeting Frank looked me over through the narrow slits of his eyes, tutted loudly and pulled a face.

'I suppose you have come here to tell me to work harder,' he said, and trained his gaze on me.

Of course that was certainly what his manager had in mind. I decided to investigate a little first. I asked him to tell me what he spent most of his time doing. He started listing all kinds of tasks, from ordering equipment to labelling bottles and also – his main task – testing various samples.

He told me how he had to spend so long on all the administration that he hardly ever seemed to have time to do his *real work*.

I talked to him about some of the criticism Terry had levelled at him. In particular that people found it hard to get a deadline out of him. Terry had said that his internal customers needed to know how long the tests he did would take, but he 'refused to tell them.' This, Terry had said, made it very difficult for colleagues to plan their work.

I asked Frank about it. He told me that he hated letting people down and the problem was that it was very hard to predict how long the tests would take for all kinds of technical reasons. So, in an attempt not to give people a date that would be wrong, he wouldn't give them a date at all. They certainly wouldn't be let down! It all seemed so obvious.

I started to explore with him his estimation skills. They were very poor. He had no idea how to do it at all.

The key with learning this skill is that you just have to start somewhere. Just guess a figure – two hours, three days, a week or whatever you think. It really does not matter how far off or how close you are.

Write down your estimate. Then undertake your task. Write down how long it really took. If you estimated half the time it really took, then, next time, just double your estimate. If you were an hour out, add another hour.

Just keep repeating the process and very quickly you will find your skill improves. What you are doing is giving yourself the feedback you need to improve your skill.

Frank and I agreed that over the next two weeks he would note down exactly how long everything he did took and we would review a fortnight later.

When I got back two weeks later, he showed me his spreadsheet. He had tabulated everything and was very pleased with the results. He went through it with me. However, there was one area that I felt concerned about. He had allocated an hour for changing a light bulb. I wondered if his manager was right after all.

I decided to ask him to explain it to me. He told me that this light bulb was in the middle of a very intricate machine. First you had to unlock the cavity with a key that was kept in a safe. Then you had to undo various plates with Allen keys. You couldn't touch the bulb with your bare hands so you had to wear gloves. The bulbs were very expensive and, for that reason, were kept in another safe on the other side of the site; some 15 minutes walk away.

Naturally several forms had to be filled out and signed before you were allowed to have one of the bulbs. I was starting to get the picture. When I checked this with one of his colleagues later in the week, asking him how long it took to change a light bulb in this machine, I was told it could easily take two hours.

Frank told me that, although he felt his estimating skills were improving, he was still very worried about making a promise to a person and letting him down if a problem arose. He just didn't know how to deal with that situation. So instead he just avoided the problem entirely. When people really pressed him for an answer he would get angry with them or come up with excuses.

I went through a simple process with him. Really it's a variation on the Five Step Approach which is explained in an excellent book, *No Fault Negotiating*, by Len Leritz. The book itself is now out of print and if you know anyone from Thorsons the publishers, please do your best to persuade them to reprint it. I have no idea why it's out of print because it's the best book on negotiation I have ever read. Every time I re-read it, I find something new.

Good old Len gives us a very easy process for dealing with these difficult situations:

First, identify the facts
'Hello, Claire, I'm sorry to have to tell you this, but you remember the work I am doing for you on compound XYZ? Well, test A has failed.'

Second, interpret the facts
'This means I will have to use another test.'

Third, the impact of the facts on the situation
'As a result of this, your results won't be ready on Friday as I had hoped.'

Fourth, the needs
'Tell me what you need to achieve...'

Fifth, the solution
'There are a number of options: I could do the quick version of test B which would give you rough results by Tuesday; I could use the long test B which would probably get you your results by Thursday, and they would be more accurate, or I could use test C. Test C is not as accurate but you would have your results by Monday afternoon. What would work best for you?'

Once Frank had this structure to use, he was much happier. It's often the case that as soon as we know a simple method for doing something, it doesn't seem so bad.

We talked a bit about his manager's perception of his behaviour. As I investigated further, I discovered that since his manager had last done Frank's job, many new regulations had been brought in. All of them meant vast increases in paperwork and administration. Some were safety requirements, some were legal requirements, others were simply now regarded as 'good practice'. The overall effect was that most tasks now took at least twice as long as they had done ten years ago.

At the end of our session Frank agreed to use the Five Step Approach and let me know how he had got on when we met up later in the month. In the meantime, I had a meeting with Terry.

I started asking Terry questions to find out what he really knew of the detail of Frank's job. He was completely unfamiliar with the new regulations and the impact of them. The equipment Frank used had not even been in existence when Terry was doing the job himself. As we discussed the situation, Terry agreed he had judged Frank harshly without finding out the facts.

He also told me that he had received some encouraging feedback about Frank's willingness to give deadlines from one or two internal customers in the last couple of weeks.

When I saw Frank again, he was delighted with the results of the Five Step Approach and said he wished he'd known about it years before.

Task-focused behaviour

Jessica complained about Ian, a manager I knew quite well.

'You go to his office,' she said, 'and he turns from his computer, never offers you a drink and then you just talk about the problem. Then, when the conversation is over, he just turns back to his computer and carries on. He never says thank you or shows you to the door or anything.'

Jessica found this very rude, offensive and difficult to deal with. It was hard for her to understand that the manager meant no offence. He had no idea how his behaviour came across.

We can all become a little task-focused at times. I have often forgotten a meal cooking in the oven when I have been working on something else, haven't set a timer to remind me. Ian was just an extreme example of this behaviour.

One of the most interesting cases like this that I have come across involved a very senior manager called Clive. He ran many technical meetings for his company, both with colleagues and with clients. He was well respected for his amazing technical expertise. Many people commented on this when I interviewed them. They all told me that he was capable of coming up with solutions during the meeting that others would have taken weeks to produce. He was highly regarded by both his colleagues and industry experts. Most of them were also scared of him.

Imagine what it would be like if you were sitting in a meeting with 14 others, working on a difficult technical issue. One of your colleagues makes a suggestion. You think it has merits. The chair of the meeting then shouts at this individual: 'How could you be so stupid?' or: 'You are an idiot.' He then goes on to explain why the suggestion is so stupid, and explains his own simple but elegant solution – berating your colleague for not thinking of it himself. How likely would you be to come up with ideas?

This is not common behaviour, but I have come across it several times. The framework for it is quite surprising. You might be led to believe that Clive behaves like this because he thinks everyone else is stupid. You would be completely wrong.

I agreed to meet up with Clive for lunch before our first coaching session. I had not met him before and was intrigued to see what he was like. I was greeted by a man who would have looked thoroughly at home wearing a dinner jacket and bow tie. I half expected him to introduce himself: 'My name's Bond, James Bond.'

Clive was extremely well turned out with highly polished shoes and well-manicured nails. He had a keen smile and even teeth.

He took me to a small Italian restaurant and we ordered what turned out to be a delicious meal.

'Have you been here before?' I asked. He smiled and admitted he had been several times.

'Is there anything you recommend?' I continued.

Clive asked me if I was vegetarian and whether there was any particular Italian dish I preferred. In the end I went with his suggestion.

Over lunch he told me some very interesting stories about his hobby – archaeology. He explained how he had first been inspired to take this up as an interest by a teacher at school. He told of his first experiences at a dig and of some of the artefacts he had found. Clive also asked me about myself and looked interested while I told him about my past.

What have we learned from this? Clive elaborated on all the areas I was interested in during our conversation. I am fascinated by archaeology and also like to hear about what motivates a person. This shows he was very sensitive to the feedback he was getting from me during our lunch. He mentioned one or two other topics which were not of great interest to me, but moved on quickly as soon as I responded to indicate this.

He even laughed at my jokes and made plenty of his own. He was witty and charming.

After a long and very enjoyable lunch, I asked Clive to tell me about some of the meetings he had had recently with his colleagues. As I have mentioned before, the stories from different parties in these situations often tally very closely. This time was no exception. Clive's description was almost word for word the same as his 'victim's'.

'Why do you think your colleagues didn't come up with the solution you worked out yourself?' I asked.

'Sheer laziness,' he answered. He did not say he thought they were idiots. In fact, his opinion was nothing to do with their level of skill; it was much more about how hard they were trying.

In his mind the technical problem he had solved was relatively simple and finding the solution was not particularly taxing. So anyone who couldn't see the solution simply was not making enough effort. He had no notion of the chasm between his level of skill in this area and that of everyone else.

'How good are you at this compared to the others?' I asked.

He shrugged. 'I'm OK,' he said straightforwardly.

'What about the others, how good are they?' I continued.

'Brian is pretty effective. Robyn lacks experience, but is competent. Gerry can be very insightful,' he replied.

Clive could see that one or two colleagues were more effective than others, but he in no way saw himself as substantially more expert than they were. To him the field was easy, so you did not need to be very skilled.

'How would you judge a person's level of skill in this area?' I asked.

'It would have to be judged by their ability to solve the problems that are presented to them, I imagine.' His tone indicated that the answer was so obvious it was hardly worth uttering.

'How long does it usually take you to solve the problems clients present?' I continued.

'A few hours at most,' he replied.

'And how long does it take the fastest of your colleagues?'

A look of astonishment filled his features. 'I don't think anyone has ever solved a client problem in less than two weeks,' he said.

He had genuinely never thought of it in those terms.

'Clive, it's not that your colleagues aren't trying. They genuinely find it more difficult than you do because you are exceptionally good at this,' I told him bluntly.

'Are you sure?' he asked.

I assured him I was. 'How can you best help them to improve their skills, then?'

'Probably not by shouting at them,' he smiled.

Clive was quite shocked to realise what he had been doing and how it had been having exactly the opposite effect from the one he wanted. When something is very clear to you, it's hard to understand why someone else can't see it.

We then started to examine the responses of his colleagues to his meeting behaviour. Clive hadn't really thought about this at all. In fact, often he did not notice it. Let's just remind ourselves of the work of Daniel Siegel. He talked about *'Sensitivity to Stimuli'*. Clive's level of sensitivity was quite low. Once he was convinced that they were not just being lazy, he agreed that there might be other more fruitful methods for encouraging his colleagues.

He had been focused completely on the task. He was unaware of the needs of his colleagues. Once I started to get him to think about them, he was able to work it out. This distinguishes him from Peter, who could not work these things out – he had to use a model from TV (Star Trek). The way Clive thought about people was mechanical and logical. It was not the way a more people-orientated person might do it, but it worked for him.

This is a very important point. I have found that when working with any of my clients you need to find a way for them to operate that builds on their strengths, not their weaknesses. It was no good to ask Clive how his team might feel when he called them idiots in front of their colleagues. This kind of reflection was not something he naturally did very well and it was not at the forefront of his mind. But I learned that when the problem was put to him, framed almost as a technical problem, then he could solve it very effectively.

So we talked about how he could most efficiently help his colleagues to improve their skill. I explained that most people learn best when they are alert but relaxed; they need to feel confident and not worry about mistakes. We identified questions that would help his colleagues to learn, rather than discourage them.

The key with these questions is the assumption behind them. If you assume the person has an idea and can solve a problem this often helps:

- What else could you do?
- What ideas do you have on this?
- What other methods could we use?
- What have you already thought of?
- What have you not thought of?
- What's important about the way we do this?
- What are the options?

You'll notice all these questions start with what. It's a very good place to start.

When you're smiling

Another problem for Clive was the lack of smiles. In a meeting he would apparently ignore or frown at any jokes or light-hearted comments from the others. This would cool down the atmosphere until it often became icy. The other people would assume he did not approve of their remarks, and they would all stop talking or making comments. The meetings dragged, and people came to see them almost as punishments. So I asked Clive what he thought about people making jokes and light-hearted comments in meetings.

'When do they do that?' he asked.

As it turned out, he had never noticed it happening. He was so focused on the task that any humour completely passed him by. I asked him if he thought it was inappropriate to make jokes in meetings.

'Not at all,' he said. He just hadn't thought about it before.

We started working on a way for him to lighten the tone of his meetings a little.

I suggested that he started smiling. He asked me when it would be appropriate for him to do that. This gave me an idea of the real size of the problem. The strange thing was that over lunch he had shown me that he was more than capable of making jokes and laughing at mine. He had told interesting and funny stories. He had also paid attention to what I had said and shown a high level of conversational skill.

I had asked him more about his holidays, and then tried out a few 'small talk' items – comments about shopping, sports and current news issues. He was more than able to discuss them. He also had a very lively sense of humour. I had tried a variety of jokes on him, some subtle, some more obvious, and he had laughed at them all.

The object with the jokes was not so much to find out if he had a sense of humour, but more to discover if he could play the appropriate social role, laughing in the right places and telling matching jokes of his own to make me feel at my ease.

It was clear that Clive was well able to hold his own in a social situation. I wondered why he did not also do it with clients. And colleagues.

Conversations are like the branches of a tree – each person can branch off from a topic as long as there is some link to the previous branch. Later, we will see an example where that did not happen. In Clive's case it all came back to his task-orientation. When he was focused on a task, he was focused on it exclusively. It was hard for him to remember to laugh. It seemed rather like people you sometimes hear of who have an awful medical condition which means they must remember to breathe. I'm sure I'd soon forget; I have trouble remembering to switch the washing machine to start once I have set the correct program.

The more I investigated, the more I realised that Clive needed some kind of mechanism to make this easy in a way that worked for him. I do quite a bit of coaching over the phone. The appointments are made for specific times. When I am working on a training course design or a book, I have learned from bitter experience that I must set an alarm to remind me, or I can miss the appointment. Even if it's a five minute job, I still need a reminder four or five minutes later. What Clive needed was some kind of reminder. I suggested that he put a note at the top of his copy of the meeting agenda, and perhaps another one half way through the agenda to remind him.

It was a considerable effort for him to focus every now and then on the people rather than the issues, whereas for many people, this behaviour comes naturally. In fact for many people, remembering to focus on the problem again is more difficult.

The good news is that Clive's behaviour improved considerably. People noticed he was smiling and that was a great relief to them. He still doesn't smile as often as most people, but it's a big improvement. His manager told me several months later that Clive had not pounced on anyone since our meeting.

I saw him in a meeting a few months later and was relieved to see he laughed at a few of the jokes. He still had a reminder on his agenda.

It's important to remember that there was never any ill intention in Clive's behaviour; he was always trying to do his best for all involved. It was the interpretation of the others' behaviour that made it seem so bad.

Needs – what do you mean, needs?
One astonishing example of this behaviour concerned Mandy. Her colleagues had all told me, with varying degrees of incredulity, about her behaviour. Each of them had described the same event:

A customer had called their helpline. Mandy had answered the call. There was no 'Hello' just a 'Yes.' Her next phrase was: 'No, I can't do that,' in a very harsh tone, and then she put the phone down.

When I had my fist meeting with Mandy, I asked her about body language.

'Body language?' she almost shouted. 'I went on a course on that – didn't understand a word of it.'

The meeting continued as we discussed the needs of other people.

'When you are in a conversation with someone, you must take their needs in to account,' I said.

'Needs, what do you mean needs?' she virtually bellowed at me.

Mandy would hardly stop talking and did not appear to listen to a word I was saying.

'Mandy, I bet you wouldn't mind if someone told you to shut up, would you?' I asked during a brief pause in her lecture.

'My friends do that all the time,' she replied without turning a hair.

This illustrates a fascinating point about many of these people; they are completely unaware of the needs of others. It isn't that they choose to ignore them. They don't even know they exist. They just plough on in their own furrow. This is why there are often no *hellos* or *goodbyes*. Greetings are mainly to do with the other person and acknowledging them. When your whole focus is exclusively on yourself, you simply don't think about anyone else. There would be no reason to even think of saying *hello*.

This puts the whole problem onto a different plane. Their behaviour becomes not the behaviour of an unreasonable person, but the behaviour of someone whose understanding of the situation is very different from yours.

Working with Mandy and her colleagues, we made huge progress. She learned how to behave effectively in meetings (something her manager had not even put on his 'wish list'), how to deal appropriately with customers on the phone, and how to be more considerate of her colleagues.

This was all done both by agreeing ground rules with the whole team, and by the team learning how to work with her more effectively. They had to forget the whole concept of embarrassment and just give her the feedback. It worked.

Too many variables

Here is a last and very different example. Andy was responsible for repairing the computers at the client's site. People found him quite frightening to deal with because he was just so 'weird'.

Andy was one of the first people I ever coached who had this behaviour. He was a young man who kept the computers in good repair on a site owned by a large corporation. It was a building where about five hundred staff worked. By all accounts Andy did a good job, technically. However, people found him very odd. The women in particular found his behaviour disquieting and, in some cases, worrying. They particularly didn't like to be alone with him.

So I went there to spend several hours on my own with him. The first thing I noticed was that his voice tone was very flat. I had never heard anyone with such a lack of tonality before and I still haven't.

His eye contact was extreme. It was far too lengthy and very direct. He did not ask me any questions about myself. None of the typical English weather questions, he did not even check whether I wanted a drink. I asked him about his job and what he did. All his answers were short and factual.

'I maintain the software and the hardware in this building. I also make recommendations on purchases. There are 532 computers and 273 printers. There were forty-two incidents last week. Thirty-five have been resolved.'

It was like talking to a very boring Mr Spock. I asked him about the people he worked with. He looked vaguely surprised.

'There are 522 people assigned to this building.'

Eventually I managed to get him talking about my computer and he gave me what I am sure, had I been able to understand it, would have been very good advice.

'Tell me what happens when someone has a problem with their computer?' I asked him. 'Take me through the process.'

'I get a phone call or an email. I look at the machine and if it's a simple software problem I usually fix it there and then. If not, I remove the equipment and return it when it is repaired.'

'What do you say to the person when you get to their office?' I persisted.

'What do you mean?' he enquired in his flat, loud voice. There was no upward movement at the end of the sentence at all, to let me know it was a question.

'Do you say: "Hello"?' I asked.

'No.'

I already knew this. It was one of the main complaints and I had been given some examples. So at least the stories were consistent.

'Imagine I have called you to look at my computer system which won't print anything,' I said. 'What would you say?'

'Where is the printer? Then I would go to the printer, check it and check the computer. Usually the printer just needs switching on.'

'But would you say: "Hello"?' I asked.

'Why?'

I suggested that he could say something like: 'Hello Nancy, I understand you have a problem with your printer. That must be very annoying for you. May I have a look at it?'

'No,' he responded.

I asked him why not. These words have lived with me ever since:

'Because it would introduce too many variables.'

This is a particularly extreme example, but you will find many of these people do not seem to engage in small talk or chat. They don't really understand what it is or what its purpose is. To everyone else this is so obvious it's hard to explain.

Since encountering Andy, I have learned a great deal about how to work with these people. I am not sure it's possible to help someone as extreme as this to learn how to do small talk. The most effective route I have discovered with this kind of behaviour is to work with the rest of the team.

Summary

Behaviours to look out for

Lack of greetings and goodbyes
This person will rarely ask how you are or how your holiday was. At the end of a conversation, he won't thank you or say how nice it was to see you either.

Very task-focused behaviour
They will be most concerned about what needs to be done and what they are doing. They will be unconcerned about the effects on other people.

Lack of awareness of others' needs
They will not ask you what you need – for example whether you might like a drink. If you don't understand something they will often fail to respond with an explanation.

Lack of awareness of others' emotions
Whether you are concerned, cross, happy or worried – their behaviour will remain the same. They will not notice how you are feeling. They will not predict how you are likely to feel as a result of what they say.

Lecturing rather than engaging in a conversation
Most conversations are made of links: each person builds on what the other has just said and links it to the subject area. These people do not link with the topics of the other person, they seem to ignore them and just continue on their own topic.

Lack of embarrassment
Most people show embarrassment when they have done something that is socially inappropriate. These people do not.

What to do
- When dealing with rhinos you need to give them *very clear* and *direct* feedback, using their name. This alone may start to change their behaviour.

- Remember to tell them what you want them to do instead of telling them what you don't want. It's much more effective. Make it *very* clear.

- *'Brian, I don't think the people next door want to hear what we are saying.'*

- *'Brian, please lower your voice, I don't want to disturb the people in the next room.'*

This may feel rather awkward to you, but it will be perfectly acceptable to them. They will usually do what you say as a result.

- **Be consistent in your feedback.** Random feedback is confusing and will lead to random behaviour. When the person does something you are pleased with – give clear feedback:

  - *'When you finished that report early it was a great help to me. It meant I had more time to prepare for my meeting.'*

  - *'That's great, thanks.'*

- **Don't be insulted** by their lack of greetings, or interest in you as a person. It's not meant to be offensive.

- **Keep your conversation to tasks** and what needs to be done.

- **If you want a change in behaviour, be as specific as you can** about what you want them to do and explain it in steps. For example:

  When a client calls with a problem:

  1 Go into his page on the database

  2 Ask the client to explain what the problem is

  3 Ask him when it first started

  4 Ask him what he needs us to do

  5 Ask him how soon he needs it to be done

  6 Enter all this information into the database

  Just saying to an insensitive person: *'Find out what the client needs'* is far too vague for him to understand.

What not to do

- **Give vague instructions or hints.** They just won't work. The person will not know what you are talking about.

- **Take offence at their behaviour.** It's not meant as an insult. You are much more likely to get upset about the situation than they are. And it won't do you any good.

Theory

The difficulty for Insensitive Behaviour people is that they do not understand hints; so you need to be direct. It is also likely that they will not feel embarrassment – so don't worry about that either.

This is because they do not have the sensitivity to pick up the feedback that most people hear or see easily. An insensitive person will not notice signals like a raised eyebrow, a nod or a change in intonation. This is just like having poor hearing or being in a room that's too dark to see anything.

Even if they did notice a feedback signal they probably would not be able to interpret it correctly, due to lack of experience. As a result of this, for most of their lives they have not had feedback on their behaviour in a form they can understand. Once the feedback is in a form they can understand, it is much more likely that they will respond.

The emotion of embarrassment is itself feedback. It is there to tell you that you have done something socially inappropriate. If you'd never felt embarrassment, how would you know when you had made a mistake?

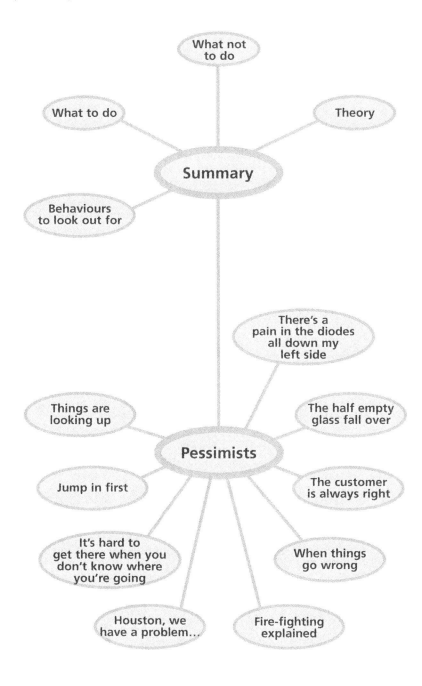

CHAPTER SIX

Pessimists

Understanding negative people

Anyone who has read The Hitchhiker's Guide to the Galaxy will remember Marvin the Paranoid Android. He was a truly negative character, always moaning and complaining about everything.

There's a pain in the diodes all down my left side

We all know negative people. What may not be obvious, however, is that the way we behave towards them often makes their behaviour worse.

I had worked with Jeremy on a number of occasions and admired his excellent management skills. He was well liked by the members of his department and a very popular, affable person.

One day he asked me to help him with a member of his team, Karen. She was very senior in the team and a particularly talented engineer. Jeremy had a new project and wanted her to take it on. She had refused. He was amazed.

I asked him to tell me what he had said to her, as closely as he could remember it.

'I said it was a great project that would raise her profile in the department. She would probably get a promotion out of it, and a substantial pay rise,' said Jeremy. 'I told her that she was easily the best person for the job, and that she had all the experience and qualifications needed.'

I groaned. I had met Karen and knew straight away that she would not respond to this strategy.

'Jeremy, you have to remember that she is motivated by solving problems,' I reminded him. 'You need to use a very negative structure and tell her about how bad the situation is,' I told him.

I suggested Jeremy asked her in this way, instead:

'Karen, we've got this project, I think we'll have to drop it because it's just too difficult. I don't think we're going to be able to do it, and I don't think we have the budget for it anyway, even if it were possible.'

Jeremy looked horrified.

'No, I couldn't possibly do that.'

'Do you want her to take on the project?' I asked.

'Yes.'

'And is she going to at the moment?'

'No,' he admitted.

'What have you got to lose, then?' I asked.

After much persuasion, Jeremy agreed to try it out. Later that day he called me to say Karen had already started on the project. He was astonished. For him this task had been almost repugnant because it was so much at odds with his usual style and understanding of the world.

Jeremy found it very hard to see anything or anyone in a negative light. Or, to put it in his words, he saw everyone in a very positive light. He looked for the best in everyone.

Let's take a look at another example:

Bethan, the senior manager in a large department, was trying to poach an old colleague from her previous company. She had heard on the grapevine that Toni's husband had been given a huge promotion, which meant they would be relocating to her area. However, she also knew that Toni didn't really want to change industries.

'I just want her to come and look around,' Toni explained over the phone. 'She'd be perfect for this job. She has all the skills we are looking for and is considered a leader in her field. I've heard that she is only considering the more long-standing companies. I want her to consider us, too.'

Toni was already expecting to be contacted by Bethan so the door was ajar if not open. I suggested to Bethan that she draft out an email and send it to me, and then we would discuss it over the phone.

Here's the email:

> **Hi Toni**
>
> **How are you? I hear you are moving over this way. We have a great job here that I know you would love and it would suit you perfectly. I am sure we could at least match your current salary and add a car into the package. And we have such wonderful facilities as well. It would be great if you could come over and see the place. Perhaps you could come and join me for lunch one day? There's some stuff I'm working on at the moment and I know you would find it very interesting. I'd be really interested to hear your views on it.**
>
> **Hope to see you soon**
>
> **Bethan**

You may be reading this email and thinking that if you ever were so lucky as to receive one like this you would be halfway to meet Bethan by now. That would show you are not like Toni.

The difference is that you look for the positive in life and see events as opportunities. Are you thinking *it sounds too good to be true* or *it just can't be that good?* Then you are closer to being Toni.

In order to appeal to Toni we had get her motivated – by identifying the pain.

We re-wrote the email:

> Hi Toni
>
> How are you? I hear you are having to leave the South.
>
> As you know I joined XXX last year. We have had some serious problems and there is one particular one that is causing havoc at the moment. I don't suppose you have any time to spare? We don't have anyone with your sort of experience, but we make up for it in lots of enthusiasm.
>
> We don't want to use the same approaches as our competitors and you do have something of a reputation in this field. We may have to accept that there is nothing we can do, but if you could spare some time to come and see me, I would be very grateful. I could show you the site and also the unit where I work. I'd like to hear your thoughts on some of the inherent problems we are facing. We are of course also looking to recruit experienced people in your field.
>
> I know you wouldn't want to move to this industry – and given all the problems, I can see why. However I thought you might like to have a look around anyway.
>
> Bethan

Bethan had a response within half an hour. Toni visited the site the following week. So how did this work?

The half empty glass falls over
Motivation is what gets you out of bed in the morning. It's what causes you to take action. We are each motivated by many different things. But we are only motivated by them in one of two ways:

• To move towards the things we like

• To move away from the things we don't like

I am sure you have heard the question: *Is the glass half-empty or half-full?* Those people who see it as half-full tend to move towards what they like, those who see it as half-empty tend to move away from what they don't like, or pain.

Let's think about the consequences of this. When you live your whole life moving towards the things you like, you will set yourself goals, be attracted to whatever you want to achieve in life, and work out how to get there. You will be constantly searching for things you will like.

When you live your life by avoiding the things you don't like, you will focus on those things, and your existence will be about searching for and solving problems. You will spend your time worrying about what might go wrong. You will be frightened of new opportunities. You will worry about what to worry about.

There are times when each of these perceptions of the world is useful and brings great benefits. And there are also times when each of them can cause problems.

People who solely move towards the things they want can be blind to problems that they meet along the way (or that they cause along the way), both for themselves and others. When I am training I often tell people that we call these 'very towards' people *the marketing department*. Whilst I am sure not all marketing people behave like this, most people seem to have met at least one marketing person who does.

The customer is always right

Years ago I worked in sales and went off on a trip to Frankfurt with my manager, the Sales and Marketing Director, Martin. He was tall and very sure of himself. I am convinced he thought of himself as charming and good-looking. I sometimes wondered if we lived in the same world.

We were visiting our German distributor. They were responsible for selling a product that delivered drugs to patients with cancer. The product was designed for them to carry around with them. The Germans were very keen to have a holster to hold it in. We already provided a leather carrying case, but they wanted a plastic holster as well.

Our engineering department had designed a product to meet this need and we had the prototype with us. At a meeting with the German sales people and their Marketing Department we showed them the holster. They were delighted with it.

Martin immediately offered them fifty holsters free. He said they could have them in the next two weeks. I was horrified. I knew that the one we had was just a prototype and that the tool to mould the production version was not even made yet. I also knew that it would take between eight and twelve weeks to get a tool made. Once the tool had been made it would probably take a couple more weeks to get the mouldings done. So the best possible delivery time was ten weeks to our factory. Then they would have to be shipped to Germany; that would add another week.

I was also aware of the costs. It was only the Germans who wanted this holster and the volumes were likely to be small. Whilst moulding them was not very expensive, the cost of the tool was high (thousands of pounds). That expense had to be borne somehow. Before working in Sales, I had been the Production Manager in the same company and knew with absolute certainty that my old boss, Jack, would be furious at the thought of giving fifty holsters away free.

I whispered to Martin that we couldn't do it in two weeks and that I also didn't think we could give fifty away free. He told me I was being very negative and continued with his promise in spite of my protests.

As I predicted, the holsters were not ready in two weeks. In fact they took fourteen weeks to arrive. Jack responded with incandescent fury when he heard what Martin had promised.

As far as Martin was concerned, the upset caused to our German distributor by our 'late delivery' was entirely the fault of the manufacturing department.

When things go wrong

People who always see the world in a negative light also create problems for themselves. What they are doing is filtering out all the positive bits, just as a positive person is filtering out all the negative bits. They are also interpreting most stimuli as threats. This means that they often do not take up what many people would see as opportunities. It also means that they tend to end up miserable.

Comments like *that will never work* and beliefs that *things always go wrong* mean that they give up long before a person with a more positive outlook, so they achieve less. This substantiates their view of the world.

Negative people tend to be most motivated when there are problems. So this is the kind of person who can be great in an emergency or crisis but lacks motivation when things are going well.

An engineer who used to work for me, Lenny, was just like this. He was tall and lean, rather like George Best, with long, glossy hair. Whenever there were problems he seemed to come alive – he worked tremendously hard and solved them quickly. But he had real trouble with long term goals.

One evening I drove home from the factory in my very old car. As I made my way down the drive I noticed a light on the dashboard. It looked like the oil was low. I pulled over and lifted up the bonnet. As I was removing the bone-dry dipstick I heard the squeal of brakes. I looked up to see Lenny's Ford Capri (complete with Starsky and Hutch go-faster stripe down the side) doing a hand-brake turn about twenty yards further on. He screeched to a halt at an angle to the kerb and leapt from the car, leaving the door open in his haste. He ran full pelt up to me.

'Nancy, Nancy, are you OK?' he shouted out with a desperate look of concern on his face. I was astonished and a little embarrassed.

'It's just low on oil, I think,' I responded. 'I haven't topped it up for a while.' I knew instantly that this was a rather stupid thing to have said.

Lenny looked disappointed.

'Sure you're OK? Should I go to the garage and get some oil?' he pleaded urgently. In the end I gave in. Who could refuse such a knight in shining armour?

So, girls, if you happen to be thinking of marrying a knight in shining armour, just check that he can set and achieve long term goals as well as respond in an emergency, before you go ahead.

Fire-fighting explained

I have often heard clients complain about people or departments that do a lot of fire fighting. This behaviour is the result of people who are motivated to act when there are problems or crises.

When this happens they all rush around solving the problem and then lose motivation, till the next problem arrives.

This means that you get a saw-tooth pattern of motivation. It goes up and down continuously. In fact, in the worst cases, people solve the same problem time and time again.

They spend time *searching* for problems. People like this find particular kinds of jobs irresistible. And I mean *irresistible*. They don't find them attractive, it's even more negative than that, they *can't resist* them.

What kinds of jobs? Well, jobs that involve solving problems: Car mechanics, research scientists, software developers, dentists and doctors (think of *preventative* medicine – why isn't it called *Medicine for Health?*) to name a few. Oh yes, and fire-fighters (whom we used to call firemen).

So if we want these kinds of people to be motivated to help us, we need to tell them that we have a problem for them to solve, and that it's really difficult. Then they will be motivated.

It's easy to make just about anyone respond in this way. Let's do it now. Imagine that your most hated relative or acquaintance is coming to stay with you for six weeks. I bet several reasons why they shouldn't come have popped into your head already.

One client I worked with found fault with everything and was very unhappy with his job. We finally negotiated a package for him and he was able to leave. He was told that, as soon as he had finished his last two reports he could go, but would still be paid till the end of the month anyway. His manager said he had never seen the guy work so fast. This was because he knew he would be able to leave – so he was motivated.

He was not motivated by going to the new opportunity that awaited him. He hardly mentioned it. All he talked about was how soon he could leave his current employer.

The situation gets bad when we have a person who is motivated by moving away from problems talking to someone who is motivated by moving towards what they want – an *away from* person and a *towards* person trying to communicate effectively.

What happens is that they each make the other more extreme. So the *towards* person becomes more *towards* and the *away from* person becomes more *away from*.

Why does this happen? Let's go back to our Marketing people for this. Imagine I am from your marketing department. I am telling you about a product we have developed. It is fantastic. Everyone in the whole world will want one. They will all buy one. All of us in this company will be millionaires many times over. This product will meet the needs of our clients so well that they will pay us lots and lots of money to have more and more of them.

Are you feeling a bit sceptical now? Most people do when they hear this. Even people who are normally quite positive will see a few flaws in the argument.

The key here is that your positive or negative perspective is only positive or negative in relation to the other person. Relative to the marketing example I have just given, virtually everyone is more *away from*, or negative.

So, to move an *away from* person to being a bit more positive, you need to be more negative than they are. For many people this is very difficult (remember Jeremy). But, with some practice, most people can manage it.

Houston, we have a problem...

I always hate early morning flights. The flight to Paris was uneventful. The taxi drive from the airport was nail biting. My taxi driver, who had met me at the meeting point in the airport, was the strong, silent type. He said nothing as we walked to the car, apart from a short comment on the weather.

We got into the car and drove off. He casually picked up one of an array of mobile phones and started a long conversation with a colleague. He held the phone with his left hand and steered with his right. Part way through this discussion, one of the other remaining phones rang. Without hesitation, he picked it up with his right hand and started to steer with his knees. I practised my Alexander Technique skills to keep myself calm, took lots of deep breaths and smiled in an effort to remain relaxed. I know you get fewer injuries if you fall and are relaxed, and I was hoping the same would hold true in a car accident.

It probably wasn't luck that got us to the client's office without incident. From his calm and confident manner, I put my safe arrival down to years of practice at knee-steering. I couldn't help wondering what would happen when the third phone rang.

Once I had arrived, I set about finding the client's offices in the new building they had moved to. There were no signs, no numbers and none of the workmen I could find had heard of the company. I asked several and they all looked completely blank. Of course this could have been down to my poor French. I decided to climb up the stairs and investigate each floor.

Finally I saw a sign I recognised and went to the door. The bell wasn't working and someone came to open it for me. It was the woman I had come to coach. She looked a little concerned, but was friendly enough.

My first meeting was with her manager, James. He had sent me the email – 'Nancy, I have a problem…' In it, he described a woman who seemed to have caused numerous problems and sounded as though she enjoyed deliberately upsetting people. In all my experience I have only once come across someone who does this kind of thing on purpose. It can look like that from outside, but that's when we are not thinking about the other person's perspective.

James described some incidents to me. People had been reduced to tears; Marie-Claire had spoken sharply to people or been rude to clients and colleagues. At first he told me that it was mainly women that had a problem with Marie-Claire. As I asked more questions it became clear that it was a wide range of people. They were all ages and from many parts of the company. However, Marie-Claire was fine with the very senior people – with the exception of her manager, the site director.

We talked about some specifics. James wanted her to do his filing (which looked as though it could do with refreshing). But when he had asked Marie-Claire to do it he was faced with dozens of reasons why she couldn't. He wanted help with letters in French. But when he asked her to help he was told that she couldn't do business letters in French. It seemed to him that all his reasonable requests were met with a barrage of reasons why they could not be met.

I asked to look at Marie-Claire's job description and was pleased to hear that she had one. I have often come across situations where they don't exist and this makes things even more difficult.

We went down the list and it turned out that there were many areas where her performance was perfectly satisfactory. It is extremely rare to find a person who is not performing in any area at all. The main areas of concern were around her dealings with others. Apparently, as the receptionist, she had *refused* to put people through. Another complaint was that she had *slammed the phone down* on a colleague.

You have to be very careful when you hear stories like this. Look at the *slamming the phone down* incident. How do you know the phone was slammed down? This complaint was second hand and made by the person on the receiving end.

When someone phones you, how could you be sure the phone has been slammed down? I think the only way would be if there had been an observer watching who saw and heard it happen from Marie-Claire's end.

All we know when a phone conversation finishes is that we are no longer connected from our end of the phone.

How do we know she refused to put people through? Only if she said: *'I refuse to put you through'* or *'I'm not going to put you through even though I know he's there'*. Or something similar.

It may well be that she said she couldn't put the caller through in a manner that was inappropriate or a bit rough. It's easy to imagine the conversation:

'Hello, can I speak to Brian Smith?'

'No.'

The *No* could mean: *No, he's not here.* Or: *No, you can't speak to him because he's in a meeting.* Of course it could mean *No, I refuse to put you through.* But we don't know that for sure. Unless she says so.

There are always at least two sides to any of these stories and that is the key to helping the people involved. You need to understand the situation from their perspective before you can help them. Otherwise it's easy to assume that they are being deliberately awkward.

After talking with James, I then spent some time with the HR people and heard about further issues and concerns from them. They had plenty of examples, all with the same thread of negativity running through them. To their credit they had gathered the specifics and talked to people to find out what had really happened. This was a tremendous help. We went for lunch before I had my meeting with Marie-Claire.

It was pouring with rain as we made our way across to the restaurant area. Over lunch they told me of their fears about tackling this problem. It was perfectly normal for them to worry that the situation would only become worse if they tackled it head-on.

When you find yourself in that position, the question to ask yourself is: *Will it become worse if we don't tackle it? And how much is it costing us?* Problems creep up on us and gradually get worse without our realising it. I call this the frog syndrome.

Although I have never carried out this experiment myself I have heard it works. If you put a frog into very hot water, what do you think it does? Jump out. Just as you or I would.

If you put a frog into cold water and gradually heat it up, guess what happens: it gets cooked.

This is the position many of us find ourselves in, when faced with the situations all through this book. We just don't notice how bad things really are because they creep up on us gradually. When this happens, it's hard to know where to draw the line. My advice is that you tackle the issue as soon as possible. It's so much easier. And cheaper.

When I first put together our Difficult Person Calculator (details at the back of this book) I could hardly believe the results myself. The calculator asks you various questions that help you to identify where the costs are with a difficult person. These range from how much of your time the person is taking up, to how many sales you may have lost as a result of having this person in your organisation.

Once we had the prototype I tried it myself using the example of someone who had worked for me and done a very poor job. I estimated the amount of my time and my colleagues' time that was taken up by the problems, and also put in a cost for the sales she should have generated, (that was her job) but didn't.

The cost came out at a staggering ten times her annual salary per year. I checked the figures twice to make sure they were correct. To my horror they were. So I have to admit that I was just as bad as the next person on this one. Then the prototype was tried out by a colleague using a real example with a current client. The cost per day of not sorting out the problem was £600 ($900).

Over lunch we talked about how to respond effectively to Marie-Claire. Effective response is a major problem for many people. They simply don't know how to deal with behaviours like this, so, what they do, unintentionally, is actively to encourage the person by giving the impression that his or her behaviour is acceptable. Or they give inconsistent random feedback. The feedback is inconsistent because they only give it when there are things they don't like. What is far more effective is to give feedback when you see the behaviour you want. A bit like you know you should when dealing with children.

Back to our friend Marie-Claire. The key points that I went over during lunch with the HR people focused on giving feedback when Marie-Claire did the things they wanted her to do. I reminded them that they must always be clear about what they wanted her to do, and how they wanted her to behave.

After lunch the session began. I was aware that Marie-Claire had told a colleague that she was not going to tell me anything, so I was prepared for her guarded approach. I was also aware that she needed to keep her job and knew that if things didn't improve she might lose it.

So, I was dealing with a person who might be feeling frightened and threatened. I knew I needed to listen to her and find out what things were like from her side.

I was confronted with a slight, elegant woman in her late fifties. She had short cropped hair that suited her very well and was dressed quite fashionably as far as I could tell (I have never managed to quite keep up with fashion, but she did look good). She had broad cheekbones and a broad jaw. Her eyes were large and clear.

Marie-Claire was smiling but looked nervous.

She told me of her travels and of her life in New Zealand and France.

She told me about her previous jobs and her wish to go into a musical career. She said she had realised in the end that she did not quite have the skills to become an opera singer. She told me how she had lost quite a bit of weight through dieting and been very successful at this. She certainly looked very trim and fit to me.

For a long time I asked questions and she told me about her life, but I didn't feel we were making a connection. Then I told her a story from my own past and suddenly, she seemed to relax and started to open up. She was clearly unhappy. With virtually every sentence she told me what she didn't want.

'I don't like my job.'

'I have no respect for my manager.'

'I can't do his filing because I never have time to sit down and do it. He never tells me what he wants. He doesn't know what he wants.' And so on.

I started to ask her what she did want. She told me what she didn't want. She seemed incapable of working out what she wanted.

This is quite a common problem. Once we are fixed on what we don't want, and what is going wrong, our mind closes to what we do want and the good parts of our life.

The research of Dr Richard J Davidson, amongst others, has shown that, if the left frontal lobes of your brain are activated, rather than the right, you will see things more positively. However, if the right frontal lobes are more activated than the left, you will see the negative.

He believes you can train yourself to see things more positively. I think he is right, but sometimes it's hard for people who have been doing it for a long time.

I think Marie-Claire was one of those people.

As we talked and I kept asking her what she wanted, I gave her some examples of how to think about what she wanted. We started with the example of the filing. She had told me that she couldn't do it because she never had enough time to sit down and do it properly.

She also complained that her manager didn't really know what he wanted (I think she might have been correct on this one). So I re-phrased:

'You need enough time to do the job properly and you need James to tell you exactly what his requirements are, then you will be able to do it.'

I encouraged her to say it herself. She found it very difficult to start with. After a few minutes she had the hang of this first phrase. As we talked I got her to rephrase everything into what she wanted, from what she didn't want. As time went on, it became easier for her. By the end of the afternoon, she was managing to do it on her own most of the time.

On the face of it this sounds like a very easy task. For some people it is very difficult. And it's no good just telling them to do it. You need to help them. It's as though there is a blind spot, an area completely invisible to them.

After three and a half hours it was time to finish. At the end of the session I asked Marie-Claire for some feedback. She was very pleased. I asked her what had helped particularly, expecting her to say it had been my skill at helping her to be more positive about life. But that wasn't it. She simply said: 'You listened to me.'

Something anyone could have done. Or was it? Most of us find it quite wearing to listen to people moaning and complaining. And, let's face it, it is very wearing when it's continuous. So we stop listening. So the people moan and complain even more in order to be heard, and we listen even less. In this way the behaviour is perpetuated.

I had left it rather late to get my taxi back and he was held up because of an accident somewhere. When he arrived I made the huge mistake of telling the driver that I was late and might miss my plane. The man looked as though he had just won the lottery. An excuse (as though one were needed) to race recklessly through the streets of Paris. It was the most terrifying journey of my life. We missed other vehicles by a hair's breadth as we hurtled through the narrow streets. He was grinning with glee and gave me a running commentary as we went, pointing out the poor driving of his fellow road-users several times.

However, I caught the plane with time to spare, having learned an important lesson about what you tell taxi drivers. He, of course, was an *away from* person. A true fire-fighter who loved to rise to a difficult challenge.

It was a while before I saw Marie-Claire again. I had often thought of her in the mean time and wondered how she was getting on. To my great relief, she had done very well.

It's hard to get there when you don't know where you're going

Her manager was very pleased and especially glad that Marie-Claire had offered to do his filing for him. When I saw Marie-Claire, I was amused to discover that, although she had offered to do the filing, she had not been able to do it because he still hadn't come back to her with his thoughts on how he wanted it.

I was asked to coach Patrick, a manager who had done very well in previous years, but seemed to have gone off track recently.

He met me in the meeting room. I was faced with someone in his thirties who had the body language of a tired old man. He was lying in his chair as though he had been dropped there. His shirt was crumpled and his face had almost as many lines.

'I assume you have some objectives for this session,' I began.

'I want you to help me find out how I have got myself into this situation and what the problem is,' he said.

'So you don't want me to help you solve it?' I enquired.

He looked at me as though he didn't understand what I had just said.

'You are aware you have a serious problem.' I said before a pause. He nodded. 'You would like me to help you find out how you got into this position and what the problem is.' He nodded again. 'But you don't actually want to solve the problem?'

At this point Patrick smiled. 'Well, yes, I suppose I want to make sure it doesn't happen again.'

I asked Patrick what he wanted to achieve. He listed out many things he didn't want and didn't like: his job, his manager, the work he was doing, having to manage the people he had to manage and the journey he had to work. Then he started talking about problems at home with his family. He had several young children, his wife had been ill, so he had been forced to take on more work in the home. He never got a moment to himself. On and on it went. I tried again, asking him what he wanted.

'I hate never getting any time to myself. I never have a moment to read or play a round of golf any more,' he complained.

'Patrick, you arrived here at nine o'clock. I asked you then what you wanted. It's now half past nine and all you have told me is what you don't want.' He looked shocked.

'Have I?' he said.

'Yes,' I told him. 'Now, what do you want?'

After a long sigh he stared blankly at me. 'I don't know,' he said.

'Think about the last time you were happy. What were you doing?' Again, there was a long pause. Then he took a deep breath.

'All I really want to do is sit and read a good book, with my favourite music on the stereo, and a glass of wine,' he told me with great sadness.

I was stunned. Not because it was an odd request, but because it was so simple. Here was a man who'd had 39 years to find a way to sit and read a good book with some music he liked whilst drinking a glass of wine – yet he hadn't achieved it yet. What could be so difficult about a goal like that? What was more, I found that I was asking myself a question: When did I last do that? I resolved to read a book that weekend.

I asked him what had happened to prevent him achieving this goal. He then told me about all the things that were wrong in his life. Not once did he talk about having a plan to achieve this goal. The reason for this was that it wasn't a goal in his mind. It was just something he had forgotten he liked to do.

We started talking about his work. He didn't like the project he was working on. I asked him what kind of project he wanted to work on.

'One that isn't like this one,' he said.

'What would a project you would enjoy working on be like?'

'Better than this one,' he answered.

'In what way would it be better?' I asked.

'It would be more challenging and more interesting.'

'What exactly do you mean by challenging and interesting?' I asked.

'A project that was in an area that was new to me and something that would be difficult to achieve.' Now we were getting somewhere. 'And with quite a few people working on it, perhaps involving some from other departments.'

I summarised his two goals so far:

'To read a book whilst listening to some of your favourite music and drinking a glass of wine; and to run a project in an area new to you, involving quite a few people, some of whom come from other departments.'

Patrick looked more cheerful than he had since he arrived. 'How many people are we talking about?' I needed to check that.

'Five or six,' he said.

'How do you think you can achieve the first one?' I asked. We started to work out what he would need; a good book (he had several, all unread), a stereo and a CD of music he liked (he had those too) and some wine. He confessed to not having much good wine in the house. We agreed that getting the wine could be his first action point.

'What about the time to do it?' I asked. He told me that this was likely to be the big stumbling block. With his young children, he was always busy. His wife had been ill so he had to do a lot of the housework.

'How much time are we talking about?' I checked with him. 'Would an hour do for starters?'

It turned out that an hour would be fine so we started working out how he could achieve that. It wasn't so difficult. The children were young so went to bed early. His wife did too, as she was still recovering. So instead of slumping in front of the TV, he just needed to do it.

Using the same principles, we identified actions he could take to get himself a project he would enjoy at work. The first action was for Patrick to spend some time defining more clearly what his ideal project would entail. The second action was to talk to his manager about it. While his manager remained unaware of Patrick's needs, how could he possibly meet them?

This is how to help someone move forwards and get away from this way of thinking. You must help them to identify what they want. They will often not be able to do it on their own. Help them to phrase it as a concrete factual statement in the positive: *I want to own a new car,* not *I don't want to have an old car.* Then you need to help them work out a plan, with easy steps, in order to achieve the goal. Lastly, you need to help them notice their progress towards the goal.

This is very important, as otherwise people can get disheartened and give up. So, in Patrick's case with his project work, his manager identified the skills Patrick needed to learn in order to get a project of the kind he wanted. They drew up a list. As Patrick learned those skills, they ticked them off the list during their regular reviews.

This visual method for identifying progress works for most people. How many of us have written things on our 'To do' list that we have already done, just so we could tick them off?

Jump in first

Here's one other little trick to try with someone who is behaving in a very negative way. Every tine I have tried it, it's worked like a dream. When someone voices an idea and your negative person takes a deep breath ready to list all his many concerns, you step in with: 'Now, let's have ten reasons why that won't work.' You need to get in before they start to speak. Usually others there will be amazed and start to laugh especially if they know the negative individual.

Strangely, the wind will have been taken out of their sails and you can carry on.

Things are looking up

Here's another strange fact. Try this little experiment. Put a pencil in your mouth and hold it so it goes across the line of your mouth just with your lips so it doesn't touch your teeth. Fold your arms and cross your legs. Frown and look down. Now think of a problem you have currently. Notice how bad it is.

After a few seconds put the pencil down, stand up and give yourself a shake. Now put the pencil back but this time hold it between your teeth so that your lips are not touching it. Relax your arms and shoulders, stand with your feet slightly apart. Take a deep breath and look up. Now think about that same problem.

What do you notice about the problem? Does it seem as bad as it did the first time? For most people, the answer is 'No'. Why is that? It's because our body language affects the way we think and perceive the world. When we are smiling we tend to see the good in life and become more open to the options available. When we are tense and looking down, we are focused inwards. We are thinking more negative thoughts. It's harder to solve problems and they seem worse.

So, a last tip for dealing with negative people is to get them to change their posture. Help them to relax and to look up. A simple way to get a person to look up is to hand them something from above when they are sitting down. Keep their attention focused upwards as much as you can.

One way to get a person to relax is to take a walk. I have used this method with several clients over the years. Sometimes I ask if they need a drink. Even if they don't I ask them to walk me to the drinks machine or fountain. With a couple of clients, where it was possible, we conducted our whole session whilst taking a walk in the country. It was easy to see an improvement in their frame of mind – and it came just from that movement.

Do be aware of your own mood, too. If you are finding a problem difficult to solve, move around and look up – you'll be amazed what a difference it can make.

Summary

Behaviours to look out for

The glass is half-empty
They see all the down sides to everything.

There are problems with everything
When you come up with a brilliant idea they immediately tell you why it won't work.

They focus on what they don't have
These are the kind of people who always tell you what they haven't got, what they can't do and what is wrong with everything.

What to do

- **The way to get them to be more positive is to be more negative than they are!**

  For example, when they say: *'This is awful.'*
  You say: *'Yes, it's terrible, I don't think we'll be able to make it.'*

  If you want to get them to do something, instead of saying:
  'This will be great – you'll love it!', you say:
  'This is probably impossible, I don't think we'll be able to do it, we haven't got anyone with the right skills and knowledge…'

  It sounds counter intuitive, but just try it.

- **In the long term, you need to help the person set goals** and identify what they want. Start with small, easily achievable goals and progress to more long-term ones.

- **Help them to monitor their progress**, so they are focusing on improvements rather than problems and setbacks.

What not to do

- **Be really positive.** The more positive you are, the more negative he will be.

- **Allow yourself to get depressed.** Sometimes these people can drag others down with them. They are so used to being like this that they don't see it as a problem. There is no route to happiness, happiness is the route. Remember to focus on the good stuff.

Theory

These people are motivated to move away from pain and things they don't like. They filter out most of the cheerful information that comes in and see only the depressing and upsetting.

Often they are so focused on what they do not want that they find it impossible to identify what they do want. This makes it hard for them to get what they want.

What really motivates this person to do something is either a serious problem or great pain. By telling them something is impossible or dreadful, you provide this motivation.

There is evidence that this is due to the right frontal lobes of the brain being more active than the left. People who are generally cheerful tend to show more activation in the left frontal lobes than the right.

Recent research seems to indicate that, with practice, this can be changed. There is quite a lot of evidence showing that meditation can help a great deal in facilitating more positive thought patterns.

CHAPTER SEVEN

Negotiating
Understanding negotiation techniques

I was on a train travelling to London. The conductor came along the carriage to check our tickets. A few seats behind me, a young man had a student ticket, but no student rail card. He was a thin, tall youth who looked to be about twenty-five. Travelling with him was a friend who did have all the correct documents.

The young man was adamant that he had bought a student rail card but had lost it. The conductor, a well-built woman in her thirties, told the passenger that he had to pay the full fare because the student ticket was only valid in conjunction with the rail card. The young man repeated his assertion that he had lost his card and had probably left it on the counter when he bought the ticket. The conductor re-stated her position.

'Are you accusing me of lying?' responded the student, in a very aggressive tone.

In the meantime our train remained motionless at Leicester station. Announcements rang out over the intercom letting us know that the train was delayed. They also apologised. By the third announcement we were given a reason: a passenger was refusing to pay his fare.

While these announcements continued, so did the discussions between the young man and what had now become a team of rail staff crammed into the narrow aisle between the seats. Not once did the passenger apologise for losing his rail card. His main strategy was to blame everyone else for everything. *Why couldn't they take his word for it? He must have had a rail card to have bought the rail ticket, wasn't that obvious? Why couldn't they phone the station where he had bought the ticket so that the kiosk staff there could look for the missing card?*

He said he had the details of the card at home; he could easily phone the rail company when he got back to England (he was hoping to catch a plane) with the details. Why didn't they just let him continue his journey in peace?

The whole negotiation consisted of both sides simply repeating their positions and becoming more and more aggressive as time went on.

Meanwhile, the train remained immobile and the chances of getting to my meeting on time were diminishing rapidly. I suspected the same was true for other passengers.

After a short intervention from a passenger (yours truly) the staff agreed to move the train and alert the police in London. In the mean time they phoned and asked the ticket office to check for the missing rail card. It could not be found.

So what is a negotiation?

In my view a negotiation is an interaction where two or more parties endeavour to discover and meet the needs of all concerned. The situation on the train was not a very effective negotiation because no one attempted to find out the needs of anyone else. The conductor stated policies and the passenger accused the conductor of not believing him. The needs of the other passengers (all of whom had paid their fares) were not even considered.

How many times have you witnessed or been involved in a similar discussion?

When a client asked me to design an assessment centre task around negotiation skills I asked him what his needs where. My client was a tall, dark, handsome Star Trek fan. We got on immediately. His name was Hugh.

Hugh worked in a new industry. He wanted me to design a task that was not specific to his industry, so that people from outside could be judged fairly alongside internal candidates. The assessment centre was a tool my client was using to test candidates for various positions. It gave them an opportunity to demonstrate a variety of skills and show whether they would be able to do the job.

After much thought, I had a conversation with an old school friend. He was a consultant anaesthetist in a large hospital. We designed the task together, based on the actual situation in his hospital at the time. It would be a tough test if you went into the situation with the wrong attitude.

We designed a role-play set in a hospital. It would involve an arrogant but highly skilled surgeon (I feel sure he was based on someone real, but never found out whom).

The situation was that you, the candidate, had recently taken up a post as a senior manager in the hospital, St Swithin's. You had tough government targets to meet. These concerned reducing waiting lists, ensuring the operating theatres were in use virtually all the time, and reducing the time a patient was kept waiting for an appointment once he or she arrived at the hospital to see a doctor.

Your attention was drawn to a senior surgeon, Dr Kildare, who was consistently failing to meet any of the targets set and seemed to be ignoring them in a cavalier attitude. Your task was to meet with Dr Kildare and persuade him to meet the targets.

You were provided with evidence about the situation, facts and figures showing how many patients had been waiting longer than the government target. In the notes you were told that you had walked past the operating theatre several times during the previous week when Dr Kildare had been scheduled to use it, only to find the theatre empty.

You had received complaints from patients who had sat for over an hour in the waiting room, and still not seen Dr Kildare (the government limit was half an hour).

Your notes gave details of Dr Kildare's surgery times and results. The time allocated to Dr Kildare to see his patients was Monday mornings.

You had half an hour to study the information and then you had your meeting with Dr Kildare. You were allowed half an hour with him and the negotiation was observed.

Many candidates started off their meeting with Dr Kildare (played by a professional actor) in a very aggressive manor. One woman in particular sticks in my memory. She was wearing a striking red outfit with an extremely short skirt. With it she had a matching pair of red stilettos and a low-cut blouse. She strode forcefully into the room and started berating Dr Kildare for all his failings. Within a matter of minutes she was shouting at Dr Kildare.

Seconds later she had leaped out of her chair and grabbed him by the lapels. As she was quite a tall woman, taller than Dr Kildare, this action resulted in him being lifted right off his feet.

I was observing this particular role-play myself and can still see her waving Dr Kildare (or the very surprised actor anyway) around much as I shake the soil off the roots of a weed I have just pulled out of a flowerbed.

Finally, the now furious Dr Kildare was released from her grip and dropped back into his chair. He sprang to his feet and started shouting at her. Dr Kildare's character had been designed to be particularly unpleasant and sarcastic in the face of an onslaught. Our actor, Nick, excelled himself. But the candidate didn't stop there.

She continued to shout and rage at him, telling him that he must meet the targets and what a poor excuse for a consultant he was. Her behaviour was in striking contrast to that of the successful candidates. They adopted a very different approach.

Their approach was to ask Dr Kildare to tell them about the problems he was experiencing. This was the key to whole exercise. Although Dr Kildare would still give you quite a lashing, on asking these questions you would discover what was really going on. The worst of it was that all the problems were your fault. Here are some of the facts:

- The operating theatres were empty because letters to patients, telling them of their operations, had not been sent out in time. There was also the problem of patients not turning up because they were ultimately too ill to have their operations. Dr Kildare had suggested to your predecessor that there should be a waiting list of people who could come in at the last moment so that the operating theatre would not be idle, but you had not done anything about it.

- Patients were left waiting for long periods of time to see Dr Kildare for a number of reasons. One of them was because the appointments that were made for Dr Kildare to see each patient were too short. He could not cover all that needed to be done in five minutes. He had repeatedly asked for more time to see patients and none had been given.

- Mondays were also a problem because during the year four of them are Bank Holidays in England. Dr Kildare lost four days of appointments due to this each year. This made up 8 per cent of his appointment time. He had asked for some other days to be made available to resolve this problem – but again, this had not been done.

As a result of these problems, the waiting lists were not meeting the government targets. By asking further, you would find out that Dr Kildare had several ideas on how the problems could be resolved and would have been happy to help.

Now, I know this was a contrived situation – but it was based on a real situation and it did give me the chance to watch probably hundreds of people deal with exactly the same situation in many different ways. And I saw the results of their efforts.

Effective negotiators

I learned a great deal from this experience. Over the months we did see a few extremely effective negotiators. The sad thing is that not one of them did anything that was particularly clever or required a great deal of intelligence. They were all skills that anyone could learn. Here's what they had in common:

Listening

They all listened carefully to Dr Kildare. They did not interrupt him.

Overall aim or needs

They focused on what all the people in the hospital were trying to achieve as a team and not just Dr Kildare.

Asking questions

They asked lots of questions to find out the facts.

Assumptions

They assumed Dr Kildare was doing his best.

Apologies

When it became clear that the fault lay with their department, they apologised.

Suggestions

They asked Dr Kildare for his suggestions.

Appreciation

They thanked Dr Kildare for his efforts.

What did the unsuccessful candidates do?

Closed mind – assumed the worst about Dr Kildare
They went in presuming that Dr Kildare was lazy and deliberately flouting the rules.

Listening
They did not listen to what Dr Kildare said and many of them shouted him down as he tried to tell them what was happening. They refused to hear his suggestions, and when he did make some they told him that they wouldn't work or, in one memorable case, they said: *'I know more about these things than you do.'*

Insults
They threw insults at him, implied all kinds of things about his professionalism and spoke rudely to him in several cases, even questioning his parentage.

Telling
They often started by telling him what to do, even though they had no experience at all in the health service.

I wonder if you recognise any of these behaviours. You might find it interesting to observe your friends and colleagues over the next few days to see if they fall into either of these categories.

Because this is a special area of interest for me, I am always on the look out for people who are effective negotiators. Whenever I see one I note down what they say and do as accurately as possible and study my notes to find out what they are doing that is so effective.

What is an effective negotiation?
In order to define this, we first need to describe exactly what we mean by *effective*. My personal view is that, at the end of a truly effective negotiation, both parties are happy and feel they have been well treated. This usually happens as a result of both parties having had their needs understood and met in some way.

Often, when I run courses on negotiation, I ask people to define what they mean by an effective negotiation. Many of them characterise an effective negotiation as one where they get what they want. They don't think about the other person. This is bullying, not what I would call true negotiation.

One of the characteristics of an effective negotiation is the *emotion* that each party is experiencing.

Emotions affect the way we think and how we use our brains. In a negotiation we need to be thinking clearly and have an open mind. When you are feeling aggressive or angry you are not using all your skills and faculties. Consequently you can end up with a poorer quality solution than necessary.

Negative emotions tend to narrow your thinking, making it harder to see the other person's point of view. You also tend to interpret their actions as threats or attacks, even when those actions are intended to be helpful. This reduces even further your chances of negotiating effectively.

There is no single foolproof negotiation style that suits all situations – but there are some basic rules that work quite well.

Recognise what you are dealing with
• Is the other person behaving like an adult or a child?
• Are they using bullying tactics?
• Are they complaining that things aren't fair?

As we grow older, our negotiation skills improve (in most cases). We learn more effective ways of negotiating as our brain matures. But some people don't, or they slip back to old childish habits.

Bullying
If the person you are dealing with is using bullying tactics, go to the chapter about bullying and use the strategies I suggest there. This is very childish behaviour and needs to be dealt with as such.

It's not fair
The person you are negotiating with may complain that things are not fair. This shows that they have progressed on from bullying, but not very far. If you have children you may have noticed the phrase *'it's not fair'* coming in at around the age of five. Other phrases may be *'she's got two sweets so I must have two'* or *'you always let him stay up till nine o'clock, why can't I?'*

Len Leritzt in his book *No Fault Negotiating* refers to this as *Scorekeeper Behaviour*. He means it's a sort of bartering. I think it's a very appropriate title, so that's what we'll stick with.

A person behaving like this will only give something if the other party gives something back. It's a trade, rather than a search for needs and a quest to meet them.

Such a person will also need clear rules and to be reprimanded when they don't obey those rules. So here is now to deal with a person behaving like this:

Agree the rules, right at the beginning
With a Scorekeeper, you need to agree the process of the negotiation. That could be something like:

1 We each state what we need and what we are trying to achieve.

2 We identify what is important to us about how it is achieved; our criteria.

3 We list all the options we can come up with between us – each listens while the other speaks.

4 We then work out which option best meets all the criteria.

5 We go with that option.

What's likely to go wrong?
Your Scorekeeper may try to cheat or not stick exactly to the rules. In this case you need to draw his attention to that transgression immediately, in the nicest possible way, and go back to the rules.

You'll find that they will accept what you say. They may stray a couple more times, but after that, you won't have much more trouble.

The way to really mess up with these people is to ignore the rules or allow them to break the rules without picking them up on it.

It's very much as though these types of negotiators are children and they just need to be told how far they can go.

Don't break the rules
I watched an interview with a world-famous author on TV. The interviewer was also world-famous and known for his aggressive questioning style. I was surprised the author had agreed to the

interview at all. Part way through the interview he asked the author how much she earned.

'I told you not to ask me that,' responded the world-famous and very rich author.

'You can't blame me for trying, though,' he responded with a childish grin.

She, quite correctly, responded with a stern look and then a smile. He did not ask her again.

Many people take umbrage when someone breaks the rules in a negotiation. Generally I don't think this is necessary. Just remind the other party what the rules are (you need to have already agreed these to do that) and carry on.

You cannot be serious

Problems often arise in negotiations because people have not correctly understood the rules, or one party has not explained them clearly enough in the first place.

A Scorekeeper may be convinced that you are trying to cheat them, so it's doubly important that you stick like glue to any rules.

I used to love watching Wimbledon when I was a child, and remember seeing John McEnroe's outbursts every time he thought a decision had been made unfairly against him. We all recognised this as childish behaviour – but McEnroe is not the only adult to behave in this way.

Making the rules clear and following them strictly is the best way to deal with these situations.

The importance of a clear process

I worked with some project managers in a multinational corporation. They had to decide on a name for a new project. You may be surprised to learn just how long it takes to make such a decision. They sent an email round to a large number of people who were involved saying something like this:

> **Dear All**
>
> **Ideas for project name**
>
> **Please send us your thoughts and ideas on the name for the new project in the logistics department.**
>
> **Tom, Dick and Harry**

A number of people responded and the team then narrowed down their choice and sent out another email:

> **Dear All**
>
> **We have drawn up a shortlist of names**
>
> **DEMON666**
> **BUNGONG555**
> **123-TOBY**
> **20-20 SPEEDUP**
>
> **Let us have your comments**
>
> **Tom, Dick and Harry**

They were flooded with complaints from people asking why their ideas weren't on the list and with suggestions for more names. There were huge battles developing between different departments, each with an axe to grind. By this stage, the name problem was now delaying the entire project. They flew people in from several countries and had a whole day of meetings about the name.

How did this happen?
They did not set their criteria and process correctly at the beginning. When I asked who was responsible for making the decision, it was clear that it was the responsibility of the team: Tom, Dick and Harry.

No one else had the authority to make the decision. The trouble was, their initial email did not make that clear.

Here's the email they should have sent:

Dear All

Logistics Project Name

We will be making the decision on the name for the new project in Logistics by 15th February. We need a name that will work with both computer systems and not be easily confused with any other projects. It must also be compatible with the accounts system so must contain three digits.

If you have any ideas please let us have them by 1st February so that we can consider them when making our decision.

We will confirm our decision to you by email on 16th February. Thank you for your help.

Tom, Dick and Harry

This email makes clear the process, and also states who is responsible for making the decision. It also provides some of the criteria for making the decision. Notice it's important to mention things like needing three digits. Some of the options in the previous email didn't meet this criterion so there was no point in even mentioning them. This means it will be easier to justify (if necessary) once it is made.

Justifying a decision
When you carry out a negotiation with another party you often have to go back to others and tell them what was agreed. This happens a lot when senior managers are making decisions and having to pass them down to more junior staff.

This is where criteria really come into their own. When you have a clear set of criteria, it is much easier to justify your decision. It's usually easier to get people to work with it too.

I have seen situations where senior managers spend ages making decisions, then they won't tell people why the decision has been made in the way that it has. Often I think it is because they don't really know themselves.

This causes dissatisfaction and distrust. It can also lead people to think that their managers just make decisions on a whim, instilling a lack of confidence in their abilities. In the worst cases people just think their managers are stupid.

Having clear criteria makes it much easier to delegate decisions, too. Where the criteria are clear, then anyone can make the decision, once they are given the circumstances and facts.

Negotiation by email

How does it feel to be on the receiving end of memos and emails? A friend gave me this example. She is a hospital consultant. A memo had recently arrived from a senior manager detailing new procedures. There was a request for comments. It seems that many of the procedures were unworkable. Some of her colleagues had sent rather aggressive comments back. This is unlikely to encourage the manager to change the procedure. How should you respond in this kind of situation? It's still a negotiation, just not one that is face to face.

You need to go back to the principles we talked about earlier. Remember the candidates in the role-play with Dr Kildare? Here are the key behaviours used by the successful candidates:

- Listening
- Overall aim or needs
- Asking questions
- Assumptions
- Apologies
- Suggestions
- Thanks

Let's see how they apply in this case. Notice how similar the principles are.

Listening

Here, this means reading the memo carefully – and not just flying off the handle because you think some parts of the new procedures won't work.

Using this example, here is a structure that will help you to get some positive results in these situations:

Appreciation

Thank the person for their letter or memo and for the opportunity to respond or give them feedback. For example:

> Dear Senior Manager
>
> Thank you for sending me the proposed new procedures to comment on, I really appreciate the chance to look at them in advance. It's good to know that you are gathering feedback before finalising the arrangements.

The aim or needs

Show that you are in agreement with the overall aim or the needs (if that is the case):

> I agree that it is extremely important we all work to reduce the waiting lists and increase the efficiency of the use of the operating theatres.

The good bits

Identify the parts you like and be specific about them:

> I was very pleased to see that you are proposing to update the form; it will be much easier to fill in.

Your concerns

Identify areas of concern and ask for suggestions:

> I notice you suggest that the operating lists should only be changed in the case of extreme emergencies. Last week I had these five situations arise, all on one day (The average each day is six).
> Patient X details of situation... Patient Y... Patient Z...

Ask questions and ask for suggestions

If you are feeling very annoyed about what the person has said, remember it was not deliberately done to upset you or make you angry. It's always useful to find out some more information in these situations:

> Please could you clarify for me which of these you think would be classified as an emergency and what you feel the criteria should be for making that decision?

Often the person who has sent the memo or email will not be familiar with some of the detail. Asking him questions about it as I have here, is a much better way of encouraging him to find out about it, than telling him they are stupid or insulting him.

Further concerns (if applicable) and request for suggestions

You can identify as many concerns as you like in this section, but it's best to stick to a few key ones. Make sure they are all formatted in this same way:

1 The facts about what the person wrote

2 Some further information if appropriate

3 A question

Here's the example in this format:

> You also suggest that the lists should be signed by the Consultant and counter-signed by XXXX by 4.30 on the previous day. As you know, many of us work at different sites two or three days every week, so we would be unlikely to be at the hospital the day before our list. What do you suggest for this situation?

This tends to come across much better than:

> We won't be able to sign the lists because we probably won't be there on the day before.

Remember, the person is trying to help – so help him.

Suggestions

Where appropriate, make some suggestions; be careful that they are gently phrased. They can follow your points of concern, but make sure they address the other person's needs as well as yours:

> I have heard there is an effective electronic signature program that could be used on electronic versions of the form if that was worth considering. I have put the web site details below. I know a manager who is using it at another hospital and would be happy to give you her details if you would like to talk to her about it.

Offer of help

Offer your services and give details of when you are available.

> I would be very happy to talk some ideas through with you on this if you have some time to spare. I will be in my office on Friday morning.

Sign off

Finish with a friendly sign off, including a second thank you.

> Thanks again for giving us all the chance to input into this document.
> Kind regards

Lastly, remember the other person is doing their best

It's all too easy to fire off an aggressive email, memo or letter. Wherever possible, leave a few hours between receiving a difficult communication and answering it. Draft out your reply using this structure and leave it for a few hours, then look again with fresh eyes or get a colleague to read it before sending it.

Planes trains and automobiles

What can you do if you are faced with a situation like the one I encountered on the train at the beginning of this chapter?

Here are some basic steps to follow:

1 Identify what must be achieved by all parties – these are the needs

2 Be careful you aren't talking about how you want it to be achieved

3 Identify what's important about how the needs are met (the criteria)

4 Come up with some options (it's best to ask the other party for their ideas first)

5 Work out which options best meet the needs and criteria of all parties – this gives you the solution

Here's an example based on the train situation:

Needs

1 Passenger – to catch his plane

2 Conductor – to make sure people pay the correct fare

3 The rest of the passengers – to reach London on time

Criteria

- Passenger – the solution is within his budget

- Conductor – the solution is within the rules

- The rest of the passengers – that the solution does not delay their journey

Some options (you can probably think of more)

Think of the options as the ways that the needs of all concerned might be met.

- Stop the train until the problem is sorted

- Passenger pays the full fare, but gets a refund if he can later prove he has a rail card

- Try to deal with the problem as the train is travelling and arrest the passenger when the train reaches London if he still hasn't paid

Now it's clear that, in the original incident, the needs of the other passengers were being ignored. Although they were not apparently part of the negotiation, the solution did have a big impact on them.

Many problems in negotiation arise because people start off by stating their preferred solution rather than looking at the needs. Then you end up bartering and each person can become entrenched in their position rather than remaining open-minded and searching for options that meet everyone's needs.

Summary

Recognising a poor negotiation
Not listening
People not listening to each other.

Negative emotions
People on either side experiencing negative emotions. This could be anger, frustration or many other emotions. Negative emotions tell us that we have an unmet need. It's often one we are not consciously aware of.

Entrenched views
Deeply entrenched views and positions. This indicates people who do not understand each other's point of view. They believe they are right and the other person is wrong.

Narrow focus
Focusing on what you're going to do, rather than on what you need to achieve. This comes from narrow thinking, which is often a symptom of negative emotions.

No criteria
No criteria for agreement. This is a very common problem, because people are often completely unaware of their own criteria.

What to do
• **Make sure you find out the needs of all concerned.** This often requires careful questioning and much listening. Where possible, write them down.

• **Identify the criteria.** This involves asking what's important about the way the needs are met. Get the criteria out in the open. You can discover them by asking: *'What's important about...(the need)?'* Then write them down.

• **Gather the options.** Get everyone's ideas. Be careful to take them all seriously. Note them down.

• **Use the criteria to sift the options.** If you find people start arguing over which option is best, go back to the criteria, or to the needs, and make sure you have got them clear. They may need refining. Very often people are not aware of their criteria or their needs, so they bring them up later in the negotiation. They often sound like the person is being unreasonable or arguing against a particular option. Use your intuition to tell you if you should check the needs or the criteria first.

- **Check the needs.** Ask them again what they want to achieve. You may need to clarify it.

- **Check the criteria.** Ask them again what's important about how the need is achieved. You may need to help them.

 ## What not to do
- **Treat them as though they are being deliberately awkward.** Just add the new criterion to the list and start sorting through the options again.

Theory

Why are so many people bad at negotiating? My view is that there are two main reasons:

- People see few examples of effective negotiation. They never even realise there are better ways of doing it.

- When people do it badly, using such tactics as bullying, they are not given feedback and taught better ways.

People are often unaware of unmet needs that they have. They experience negative emotions for years, without realising what the emotion is telling them – that they have an unmet need. An effective negotiator can help them to identify what these needs may be. Once the need has been identified, it is much easier to meet.

I have yet to meet the person who deliberately negotiates in an ineffective way. Given help, virtually everyone can improve their negotiation skills, and we would all be much happier if that were to happen, wouldn't we?

Quiz

You have now met six different kinds of difficult people:

Rhinos
Insensitive people who do not notice the kind of stimuli that most other people do.

Cry babies
Emotional people; people who respond to situations with buckets of emotion and need to be connected to everyone else.

Bullies
People who bully others and focus only on their own needs.

Ditherers
Indecisive people; I couldn't decide whether to include that one or not, I thought it might be useful but then I wasn't sure…

Fusspots
Detail-orientated people who focus on a very small part of the world and don't see the big picture.

Pessimists
Negative people who run their lives by avoiding what they don't want, and fire-fighting, if they are motivated enough.

Test yourself here by having a go at our quiz.

1   Which people behave as though they are looking at the world through a long cardboard tube?

2   What is the key to getting indecisive people to make a decision?

3   Can you change the behaviour of an insensitive person? If so, how?

4   How do you motivate a seriously negative person?

5   Which profile can easily encourage bullying and why?

6   How have I managed to offend large numbers of emotional people?

7   What do you think are your own tendencies?

8   Which difficult behaviours do you tend to run into most often? What does this tell you about yourself?

9   How would you give instructions to a person who was very detail-orientated?

10 How would you discuss a problem with a very emotional person?

11 Identify three things effective negotiators do.

12 Identify a difficult person you know and which categories he or she fits into (there may be more than one category).

Please email your answers to info@vinehouse.co.uk and, if they are correct, we will send you a **free** CD.

Understanding

The most important thing to remember when you are dealing with a difficult person is to make every effort to understand him or her. After all, every one of us can be difficult at times. Once you have an understanding of the other person's perspective, things get much easier.

Remember, they are not deliberately making your life more difficult. In fact, they manage to make your life more difficult with no effort at all. Very probably you are inadvertently making every effort to enable them, and encourage their behaviour. Usually, if you change the way you behave towards a difficult person, his or her behaviour will change.

The key then, is to know how to change your own behaviour. You have read this book, so you should now have exactly the information you need.

As you know, I have worked in this field for many years and have seen some startling changes in people taking place before my eyes. Of course there have been a few failures, but I like to think there are fewer now than when I started.

As I have developed techniques and learned about what drives people to behave in the way they do, I have managed to find quicker and easier ways of resolving the problems. The techniques in this book are the results of this research. Every technique in this book has been used many times and found to work. Try them out for yourself and, if you're still having problems, contact me.

I would be pleased to hear about your successes, too.

Bibliography

Charvet, Shelle Rose, *Words that Change Minds*, Kendall/Hunt Publishing Company

Damasio, Antonio, *The Feeling of What Happens*, William Heinmann

Dilts, Robert, *Slight of Mouths*, Meta Publications

Laborde, Genie Z, *Influencing with Integrity*, Syntony

Leritz, Len, *No Fault Negotiating*, Thoresons

Misino, Dominick J, *Negotiating Without a Net*, Harvard Business Review, October 2002

Pinker, Stephen, *How the Mind Works*, Penguin

Ratey, John J, *Shadow Syndromes*, Bantam Trade Paperback

Robert B. Cialdini, *Influence, Science and Practice*, Allyn and Beacon

Rosenberg, Marshall B, *Nonviolent Communication*, PuddleDancer Press

Seagal, Sandra, Horne, David, *Human Dynamics*, Pegasus

Siegel, Daniel J, *The Developing Mind*, Guilford

Tannen, Deborah, *You Just Don't Understand*, Virago

Appendix

Here is a list of emotions in case you are dealing with a very emotional person and find it hard to think of emotions off the top of your head. It's really useful to sprinkle them into letters and emails to emotional people. Having a list makes life so much easier.

Emotions

abandoned	chagrined	downcast
absorbed	cheated	downhearted
abused	cheerful	dull
adventurous	coerced	eager
affectionate	cold	ebullient
afraid	comfortable	ecstatic
aggravated	composed	edgy
agitated	concerned	effervescent
alarmed	confident	elated
alert	confused	embarrassed
alive	contented	embittered
amazed	cool	enchanted
amused	cornered	encouraged
angry	cross	energetic
anguished	curious	enlivened
animated	dazzled	exasperated
annoyed	dejected	excited
anxious	delighted	exhausted
apathetic	depressed	exhilarated
apprehensive	despairing	expansive
ashamed	despondent	expectant
astonished	detached	exultant
attacked	diminished	fascinated
beat	disaffected	fatigued
betrayed	disappointed	fearful
bewildered	discouraged	fidgety
bitter	disenchanted	forlorn
blissful	disgruntled	frightened
breathless	disheartened	frustrated
broken-hearted	dismayed	fulfilled
bullied	displeased	furious
buoyant	distressed	glad
calm	distrusted	gleeful
carefree	disturbed	gloomy

glorious	miserable	shocked
glowing	misunderstood	sleepy
good-humoured	morose	sorrowful
grateful	mournful	sorry
guilty	moved	spiritless
happy	neglected	splendid
harried	nervous	startled
heavy	nettled	stimulated
helpful	numb	surprised
helpless	optimistic	suspicious
hopeful	overjoyed	tender
hopeless	overwhelmed	tepid
horrible	overworked	terrified
horrified	panicky	thankful
hostile	passive	threatened
impatient	peaceful	thrilled
indifferent	perky	tired
inquisitive	perplexed	touched
inspired	pessimistic	tranquil
intense	pleasant	troubled
intense	pleased	trusting
interested	pressured	uncomfortable
intimidated	proud	unconcerned
intrigued	provoked	uneasy
involved	put down	unhappy
irate	puzzled	unnerved
irked	quiet	unsteady
irritated	radiant	unsupported
jealous	rancorous	upset
jittery	refreshed	uptight
joyful	relaxed	used
jubilant	relieved	vexed
lazy	reluctant	warm
let down	repelled	weary
lethargic	resentful	wistful
listless	restless	withdrawn
lonely	sad	woeful
loving	satisfied	wonderful
mad	scared	worried
manipulated	secure	wretched
mean	sensitive	zestful
mellow	serene	
merry	shaky	

Contact Nancy Slessenger

To find out more about our services:

- Taking the pain out of writing objectives
- Optimising people's performance using latest brain research
- Handling difficult behaviours quickly and effectively
- Developing successful communications skills and strategies

contact:
Vine House essential Ltd
Hawthorn Cottage
Guildford Road
Normandy
Surrey
GU3 2AW
United Kingdom

+44 (0)7071 224569

www.vinehouse.co.uk
email info@vinehouse.co.uk

To register for the eZine *Challenging People*, or to download free reports and articles and to access *The Difficult Person Calculator* go to www.vinehouse.co.uk

Other Vinehouse publications available:

- *How to Write Objectives that Work*
- *Praise and the Appraisal*
- *Feedback for the Fainthearted*
- *The Lazy Person's Guide to Time Management*
- *The Quick Guide to Dealing with Difficult People*
- *How to Interview Successfully*
- *Memory Tips for Teachers*
- *Brain Magic* (book and CD set)
- *Lion Taming for Beginners* (Bullying CD and Podcast)